LIVING LEGACY

Stories of a Restaurant Family

FEATURING RECIPES FROM
CHEF BILLY MCCALLUM

Molly McCallum

WIT & THYME
PRESS

WIT & THYME
PRESS

copyright © 2023 Molly McCallum

photography copyright © 2023 Molly McCallum

All rights reserved. No part of this book may be reproduced or used in any manner without the prior written permission of the copyright owner.

To request permissions, contact molly@witandthyme.com

ISBN: 979-8-9882004-0-6

Photographs by Molly McCallum unless otherwise noted.

Cover design by Molly McCallum

Wit & Thyme
834 Northwest Fort Clatsop Street
Bend, Oregon 97703
www.witandthyme.com

Disclaimer: These are my memories from my perspective, and I have tried to represent events as faithfully as possible.

For Bill & Betty

"Before I got married I had six theories about raising children;
now I have six children and no theories."

John Wilmot

Author's Note

I began with a stack of handwritten and typed recipes Chef Billy had compiled over the years and some Treehouse menus. With the exception of a few dishes Billy made at his home, I prepared each recipe in my Bend, Oregon kitchen, scaling most of them down to two to six servings from the extra-large batches used at the restaurant. Some of the menu items weren't in written recipes, so I relied on memory, both Billy's and mine, and the menu description to recreate those dishes.

Over the past couple of years, my family graciously waited while I photographed each entrée, salad, dessert, etc., then served up memories for my husband, Bob, and me, and new favorites for our daughters, Ella and Hailey. Friends were very helpful in taking extras when we couldn't (or shouldn't) possibly finish another rich cheesecake or pasta dish.

I've included detailed instructions with every recipe in hopes that those of you who are less experienced cooks can prepare them with confidence. I've also modified some ingredients that make more sense for the home kitchen. Don't hesitate to use shortcuts. You certainly don't have to make your own croutons for Caeser Salad, and I'll admit to not always marinating my chicken before making Chicken Piccata. You should give yourself a pat on the back for any effort to cook at home!

It has brought me great joy to do this work and solace as I've grieved the loss of my sweet husband, who passed just over a year ago. Nothing is more important than our connection with loved ones, and few things deliver comfort and reminders of those we've lost like a familiar meal can.

My niece, Alicia, said this book is like a love letter to our family. That has been my intention, though I hadn't put it in words. Our family deserves a love letter.
Every family does.

Be well and enjoy!

Molly

INTRODUCTION
12

BREADS & COFFEE CAKE
21

EGGS & GRIDDLE
37

SALADS & DRESSINGS
53

SOUP DU JOUR
67

SAUCES, SEASONINGS, & MARINADES
81

SANDWICHES & WRAPS
93

APPETIZERS
107

SIDE DISHES
121

PASTA
131

SEAFOOD & LAKE FISH
145

CHICKEN & PORK
165

BEEF & LAMB
181

DESSERTS
195

CAKES, FROSTINGS, & CHEESECAKES
213

PIES & TURNOVERS
239

The McCallum family
Left to right; Betty, Bill. Pat, Molly, Mike, Suzanne
Seated; Billy, Cindy

When Bill McCallum realized his dream of opening a restaurant, he intentionally established a legacy for his six children.

He couldn't send us all to college, but he gave us a training ground to learn many life skills and lessons that we could never have attained through formal education. Sadly, at fifty-eight years old, we lost our dad to cancer in 1989. He only lived to see twelve years of the restaurant's twenty-year run, but what he set in motion made indelible marks on each of our lives. We remain a restaurant family, though most of us don't work in the industry anymore. It's simply who we are.

Our dad, along with our mom, Betty, and friends Jim and Sharon Cisler, opened the Treehouse restaurant in Eugene, Oregon, on the eve of Thanksgiving in 1977. As a traveling salesman, Dad developed a passion for fine dining in big cities like Chicago, San Francisco, and nearby Portland, where he and my mom favored seafood and steak houses like Jake's Famous Crawfish and RingSide Steakhouse. Dad and Jim's charismatic personalities and focus on hospitality came together to create a place patrons fondly recall twenty-five years after the last dinner was served. Food memories can evoke deep emotions, and I hope this book reignites the best ones. To those who never had the pleasure of dining at the Treehouse, I invite you to try the recipes and make your own special memories.

Located near the beautiful University of Oregon campus, the Treehouse was among a handful of restaurants in Eugene known for fine dining. It was one of the top choices for special occasion dinners, business lunches, and leisurely weekend brunch. Valley River Inn and North Bank had lovely views of the Willamette river. Oregon Electric Station had a historical vibe and more of a big-city atmosphere with a lively bar scene. The Excelsior was a charming French cafe in the heart of campus. (I can still taste the incredible pot de crème they served garnished with a toasted espresso bean.) And Chef Willie had a restaurant focused on the finest local ingredients with a French flair. After Dad passed, Mom enjoyed taking herself out to dinner, and Willie's was her favorite place to go. They all had exceptional food, cocktails, and ever-expanding wine menus as Oregon wine country made a name for itself in the 1980s.

Pat McCallum and Jim Cisler in the Treehouse dining room

The Treehouse didn't have river views, nor was it located in a particularly hip or historical setting. Still, it had something that set it apart from the rest and drew customers from all over the Pacific Northwest: Dinner theater!

Dad and Jim were friendly with a local director named Ed Raggazino. Dad had worked as a production assistant to his good friend, John Fabian, on the cult classic movie Sasquatch: The Legend of Bigfoot, and Ed was the director. Dad and Jim also worked together on a film called Buffalo Rider as writers and researchers. Their film careers were short-lived but fruitful in bringing about a great partnership. Together, they came up with the idea to produce quarterly dinner shows called Elegant Evenings. The Treehouse kitchen created four courses of fabulous cuisine, and Ed directed talented local performers to do two sets of singing and dancing, bringing a taste of Broadway to Eugene. They were wildly popular, especially when Dad and Jim, both great singers, and other staff members, including a few of my siblings, joined in the acts.

Getting all dressed up and attending those evenings was a true privilege of my childhood. Because of them, I fell in love with the music of Cole Porter, Steven Sondheim, Rodgers, Hart, and Hammerstein, and countless show tunes. I always think of the song "If They Could See Me Now" from Sweet Charity as an unofficial theme song for the Elegant Evenings. "We're eatin' fancy chow and drinkin' fancy wine," was shouted joyously from the audience as they sang along with the performers in one of the shows.

Jim Cisler, Bill McCallum, and Danny Kelsay aka The Scarecrow, Cowardly Lion, and Tin Man from "Elegant Evening Goes to the Movies"

For everyday dining, freshly prepared seafood, hearty steaks, and a wide range of uniquely prepared entrées brought people in and kept them coming back. The decor and ambiance throughout the restaurant reflected our mom's elegant style and good taste. She insisted on spotless glassware, polished silverware, and clean white linens. At home, she would have my sister, Suzanne, and I painstakingly polish each piece of the "good silver" knives, forks, spoons, and iron linens before holiday meals. Luckily, the Treehouse had the stainless-steel variety, but it was still thoroughly checked by the waitstaff for cleanliness. Nothing less would do. The white linen tablecloths and napkins were laundered and pressed daily by a linen service, and then the napkins were folded into fans by the waitstaff, bussers, and me when anyone caught me standing around with nothing to do. "Go fold napkins" was an oft-repeated command.

There was a single stem of a rose or carnation in a crystal bud vase on each table, and fresh-cut bouquets adorned the front desk and antique breakfronts that held extra glassware on the main dining and upstairs floors. Every Friday was flower day, and Mom would go to the flower market across town to pick out fresh roses, baby's breath, and other seasonal flowers to take back to the restaurant. There she would arrange each bud vase and bouquet by hand. She was a natural at making things beautiful.

I often went with her on her Friday flower runs. I remember the smell of freshly cut flowers in large white buckets in the walk-in coolers at the flower market, and I loved helping her pick them out. When we returned to the restaurant, we would haul them to the upstairs kitchen, which housed the bakery, where I would eventually spend most of my time. I would pull leaves off and cut the stems of the roses at an angle as she taught me. As I grew older, I even got to put together arrangements myself. The best part of the day, though, was the midday break for milkshakes to reward ourselves for all our hard work. Always strawberry for mom, chocolate for me. My niece, Sara, later had the privilege of making the same Friday afternoon memories with her Grandma Betty, and we talk about her love for strawberry milkshakes every time we see a Baskin-Robbins.

Along with the fresh flowers, Mom took care of the many potted plants and trees that complemented the rattan chairs, floral tapestry upholstery, and wicker accents that created the ambiance at the Treehouse. Wednesday was plant-watering day, and I was the prime candidate to help with that as well. It beat scraping the gum from underneath the dining tables with a dinner knife (one of my earliest and least favorite jobs).

She also chose the classical music that played during brunch, lunch, and dinner service. Mom was an accomplished violinist, and music was a passion of hers. Vivaldi's *Four Seasons* was a favorite, and she loved George Winston's *December* to play around the holidays. The bright, lively, sophisticated music set the tone for fine dining and never played so loudly that it would overpower the guests' conversations.

Mom preferred behind-the-scenes work; I'm like her in that way. It took her a few years to grow comfortable with her front-of-the-house role as hostess, but she did so graciously and tirelessly, still putting in sixty-hour weeks at age sixty-eight when the restaurant closed in 1997.

Betty McCallum, at the Treehouse front desk

Bill McCallum, in the Skylight Lounge

Dad was in his element at work,

welcoming people, whether he was on hosting duty or just onsite, floating around to ensure everything was running smoothly in the kitchen, bar, and dining rooms. He made people feel like they were among his closest friends; he was handsome and charming to the ladies and amusingly irreverent with the gentlemen. If Dad didn't have an apron strapped on to help with prep or expedite orders in the kitchen, we would find him pulling up a chair to chat with guests in the dining room or sharing a scotch and a story with the regulars at the bar. It was excruciating for painfully-shy me to be seen in public with him because everyone knew Bill McCallum, though he often had no clue who he was talking to outside the restaurant walls. This was not due to insincerity; he truly loved people, and when you were in his orbit, you had his full attention. Jim Cisler has a similarly magnetic personality, and many customers initially drawn in by the cuisine became regulars who came to see the two of them; the food was a bonus.

My siblings and I range widely in age and personality, so our experiences in the restaurant were unique. One thing we had in common was we had an unspoken sense of duty to give at least a few years of our time to Dad and Mom's endeavors. They worked hard to provide us with the best life possible. There was never much extra money; more often, there was not enough, but they never put that worry on us. We were always well-fed and cared for. They ensured we had a good education at St. Paul's Catholic elementary school and Marist Catholic high school, no doubt paying only what they could and counting on scholarships.

Cindy is the oldest and, at twenty-one, was grown and out of the house when the restaurant opened.

She worked as a waitress in the dining room and lounge in the early years, but it was a relatively short stint compared to the rest of us. Ready to move forward with her life, she moved out of Eugene in the early 1980s. Whenever Cindy recalls her time at the Treehouse, she talks about the countless times she quit or our brother Mike fired her. Either way, her cocktail-waitressing apron or something else was thrown at him. Our dad would have to step in to tell Mike he didn't have the authority and tell Cindy she needed to get back to work. I can only imagine the patience it took to manage those two working together. Mike is one year younger but, back then, liked to consider himself more mature. He felt his duty was to keep his free-spirited, rebellious sister in line. (He has long since given up that effort.) He loves to tell the story of conspiring with the principal at Marist ,when he was a junior and Cindy a senior, to make sure she graduated. It saved them the trouble of putting up with her rebellion for one more year and her the trouble of continuing to attend high school.

1972 Billy, Cindy, Mike, Pat (aka "Joe Cool)
Front: Suzanne, Molly

Cindy and Mike still occasionally quarrel, but it's mainly for the amusement of their nieces and nephews at family gatherings. Their love for each other is stronger than any practical or philosophical disagreements. We credit Bill and Betty for instilling the value of unconditional love. No matter our differences, and we are all quite different, it was simply never an option to cease communication or refuse to interact with each other. I came to greatly appreciate it as I got older and realized that isn't the case in many families where bonds break and families become fractured.

Michael made an early and natural move into a managerial position at the restaurant after paying his dues in the dishwashing room, waiting tables, and putting in some time as manager at Papa's Pizza. His innate leadership qualities and organizational skills were exercised in the dynamic environment of the busy restaurant and provided an invaluable education that led him to his more permanent career. In the late 1980s, Mike took a job with the Oregon Restaurant Association, where he worked to benefit restaurants statewide. Several years later, he moved to the National Restaurant Association, where he served as a vice president.

It was a good move for him to put his skills to use on a larger scale than in the family restaurant. And, as much as I love him, I'm sort of glad I didn't have to work for him. All I remember from back then was him yelling at me for stealing chocolate from the bakery when I was a child (to be fair, I was a repeat offender). The ability of big brothers to devastate little sisters should never be underestimated. Instead, I have enjoyed the best part of him. He walked me down the aisle when I married my husband, Bob, as a stand-in for our late father. He has also come to my rescue countless times and is a caring and protective uncle to my daughters, Ella and Hailey. Behind that tough exterior is a heart of pure gold.

Patrick is the third of the "Irish triplets" born to Mom and Dad from 1956 to 1958. (They really showed mom's doctor. She almost called off the wedding when he told her it was doubtful she and my dad would bear children.) His sensitive and charming but practical nature lends itself beautifully to his work. He began his restaurant career bussing tables at a Mr. Steak restaurant and was ready to step into a role waiting tables at the Treehouse when it opened. He quickly became the head waiter and, later, took on managerial positions. Pat's life's work has centered around hospitality. He has endured as one of Eugene's most consistent restaurant operators and caterers from his time at the Wild Duck in the late 1990s to the present day with Mac's Nightclub and Restaurant and McCallum's Custom Catering.

William Thomas McCallum, or Billy, as we call him, was born in 1961, the fourth of Bill and Betty's children. He is not only our dad's namesake (though not a junior, they had different middle names) but also his spitting image. My aunts and uncles would refer to him as "Little Bill," and the comparisons to dad were never-ending. He shared his passion for food and cooking, finding his way around the family kitchen long before the restaurant years. He was just sixteen when the Treehouse opened but quickly made his way to head chef, soon after graduating high school.

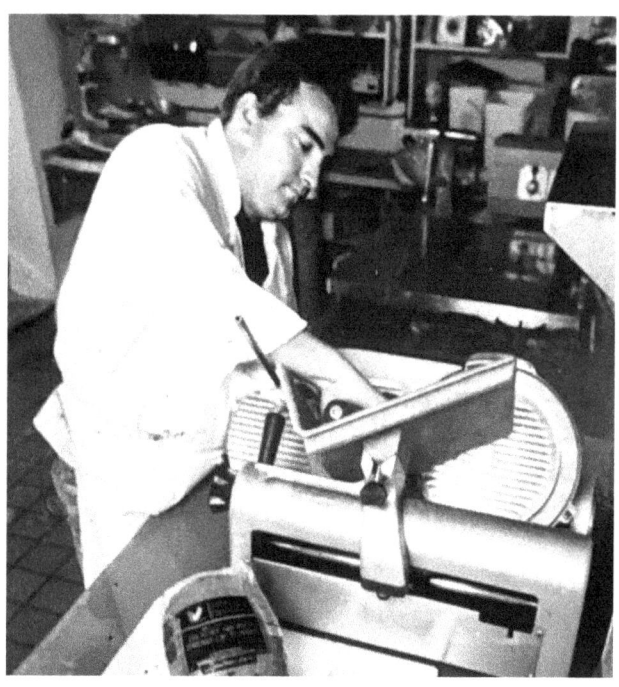

Billy has the quintessential qualities of a chef. He is deeply interested in eating, preparing, and talking about food. Most importantly, he loves to feed people. His gregarious personality allows him to connect with customers when he comes out from behind the line, conveying pride and love of his work combined with a genuine appreciation of their patronage that makes the food taste even better. Most of the recipes in this cookbook were created and perfected by him and enjoyed in Eugene for the past forty years.

After the Treehouse closed, Billy and Pat opened Mac's Nightclub and Restaurant, Billy Mac's Bar and Grill, and McCallum's Custom Catering. It's wise to know your limits when it comes to partnerships, and in 2009, the two of them decided to part ways and, in their words, "just be brothers." Pat kept his nightclub, Billy his neighborhood bar and grill, and both continued to offer catering in town, often referring jobs to each other that they couldn't take or thought were best suited to the other. Their amicable parting has served them both well and allowed them to remain the best of friends and brothers.

Suzanne is the fifth sibling and was thirteen when the Treehouse opened. She bussed tables throughout high school and eventually started waitressing. Like our older sister, Cindy, her passion does not lie in the restaurant industry. She is a gifted singer and guitar player, and that has been her life's constant focus. She and her husband, Peter, have worked as caregivers over the years, and they continue to perform music together in Eugene and surrounding areas in bars and venues like Mac's Nightclub and Restaurant.

Suzanne and I sang together in the basement bar at The Treehouse, aptly called The Root Cellar Lounge, in the mid-1980s when I was in high school. On Thursday nights, she would play her guitar, and we would sing songs like "Watching the River Run" by Loggins & Messina, "Grandpa" by The Judds, and "Sweet Baby James" by James Taylor. I remember feeling slightly embarrassed but mostly amused when the Marist Brothers who taught at my high school would be at the bar, probably thinking I should be home studying, but maybe they could see my heart wasn't in my schoolwork.

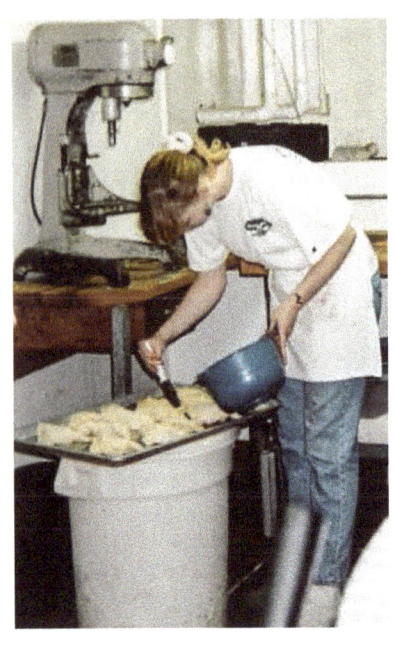

Finally, there's me, Molly, born last in 1969. As the youngest and quietest (with Suzanne a close second), I was a constant observer and spy of the family. My mom told me I brought a calming force to the household when I was born. My five siblings ranged in age from four to thirteen years old, and handing a cute baby to a cranky adolescent was a quick way to tame their mood. I naturally and unconsciously took on the role of peacemaker and brought that into my work at the restaurant. I took pride in my ability to cool the tempers that inevitably flared between the waitstaff and kitchen from my post in the bakery or when working the salad and sauté station on the kitchen line.

At eight years old in 1977, it's no exaggeration to say I grew up in a restaurant. It was an accelerated upbringing, for sure. Not only was I the youngest of six siblings, but I also became the adopted little sister to the many waiters, waitresses, cooks, and dishwashers who worked at the Treehouse. Most of them were students at the U of O. They confided in me and provided me with way too much knowledge of the inner workings of the twenty-something crowd. It wasn't always due to their questionable judgment; I could make myself practically invisible to eavesdrop on adult conversations. I had trouble relating to my peers and remained painfully shy at school, but I found my voice at the restaurant and broadened my study of the adult world that I was so eager to enter. I often say I can't imagine raising my own children the same way, but I wouldn't trade my experience for anything.

In addition to the restaurant and family, the things most important to our parents were spending time outdoors, music, and their Catholic faith. Our family vacations were usually spent on the Oregon coast for spring break and two weeks tent camping every summer at Three Creeks Lake, just outside Sisters, Oregon, which is still our favorite gathering place. My siblings play their guitars, and we all sing around the campfire as we did decades ago, though we don't stay up quite as late as we did in the 1970s and '80s. Back then, I would always worry we were bothering the other campers, but they often wandered over to listen, sometimes even join in, or thank us the following morning for the beautiful music.

As you might expect, our camp food is a little over the top; no hot dogs for our crew. Steaks, kabobs, salmon pâté, and pan-fried oysters are more my brothers' speed, along with fresh Brook or Rainbow trout if the fishing is good. (When my husband and I started camping on our own, I began to appreciate the simplicity of hot dogs and hamburgers, especially when our daughters were very young. Camping is a lot of work! I don't know how my mom managed with so many of us.)

2013 Billy, Pat, Mike
seated: Suzanne, Molly, Cindy

August 1990
Three Creeks Lake
Left to right: Steven, Pat, Bob, Molly, Sara, Billy, Cindy, Randy, Rachell, Betty, Mike
Left to right, seated: Suzanne, Linda, Nancy, Gretchen, Bella (dog)
Left to right on laps: Abby, Alicia, John

Mom's faith and passion for music led her to direct the folk group that played at church for many years. She was a bit of a renegade bringing in contemporary music to replace the traditional organ and choir hymns. Despite a little pushback from the older crowd, she loved involving and working with young people, and most parishioners welcomed the change. My siblings and I participated every Sunday, at least in our teenage years, singing and playing tambourines or guitars.

When our dad passed away, we were all devastated, but we did what our mom taught us. The six of us stood up and sang together in St. Paul's Catholic church in front of a standing-room-only congregation. The song we ended with was Dan Fogelberg's "Leader of the Band." My brothers had learned it a few years earlier to sing around the campfire, and my dad loved it. He fancied himself the subject of the song, as we all did. We were shaky with emotion as we sang, but we held each other up, singing strong when one of us broke down, full of love and respect for our dad. Ten years later, at our mom's funeral, we ended with a recording of her playing "The Tennessee Waltz" on her violin. It was a moving tribute to a beautiful, talented lady.

Each of my siblings and I are living legacies to Bill and Betty, the leaders of our band. The qualities that made the Treehouse special came from our family and the Cisler family's shared interests, values, and traditions.

This book celebrates the beautiful food and memories we've created over the years. As you enjoy the recipes and stories, I hope you feel like you've been welcomed into our restaurant family.

BREADS & COFFEE CAKE

Grandma's Rolls 25

Cinnamon Rolls 26

Sour Cream & Pecan Coffee Cake 29

Banana Bread 30

Date Nut Bread 31

Focaccia 32

Croutons 34

Garlic Crostini 35

When I run into people who remember the Treehouse, they might mention different favorite dishes like Whiskey Cured Prime Rib, Tillamook Cheddar Cheese Soup, or Mudd Pie. The one thing, however, that they always want to talk about is "those rolls!".

Our Grandma McCallum's sweet, soft dinner rolls became legendary in Eugene when we served a hot basketful before every meal at the restaurant.

The woman behind the dinner rolls is the real legend in our family. I had the privilege of knowing Ina McCallum, my dad's mom, for sixteen precious years, and she personified everything a grandmother should be. When I was in grade school, a friend complained about her grandmother's short temper, and I was in disbelief. I never heard mine say a harsh word to anyone, especially not any of her grandchildren. She made each one of us feel like we were her favorite.

In the summer of 1923, Ina was thirty-one years old and pregnant with my Aunt Louise when she and her husband made the long journey from Idaho to Bend, Oregon, with their two young sons. Robert McCallum was a stuborn Scotsman who would not eat any bread his wife didn't bake, so she would bake fresh loaves as they camped along the way. My uncles, Lewis and Hoyle, recalled having to hold a metal box that would radiate heat to bake the bread. I marvel at the thought of her, pregnant, tired, and undoubtedly hot, traveling across the high desert. Baking bread and fixing breakfast, lunch, and dinner for her family on the road. She was a genuinely selfless and incredibly strong woman.

By the time I was born in 1969, Grandpa and Grandma had lived a long, hard-working life and were retired in a little white house near my aunt and uncle. My sister, Suzanne, and I have lovely memories of visiting Bend, where Grandma would walk us to Pioneer Park with a bag of old bread to feed the ducks. (Long before it was a banned practice.) She loved the ducks and would draw me pictures of them with her gnarled, arthritic, tremoring hands. Even into her eighties, she still had a pan of hot, fresh rolls in her kitchen every day, sometimes topped with vanilla icing because she knew how much we loved sweets.

When I turned fourteen, I began baking Grandma's rolls at the Treehouse after school. It made me proud to share them with so many people. They were never as good as hers, but they still made the best breadbasket in Eugene. For several years after I had stopped working at the restaurant, I would wake up in a panic, having dreamt we ran out of rolls on a busy night. I make them a few times a year in my kitchen in Bend, where I've lived for twenty years. It's meaningful for me to live and raise my daughters where my dad grew up, and some of my fondest memories were formed; I only wish we could still visit Grandma in her little white house.

As Grandma would say, I'm "pleased as punch" to share her recipe with you.

I encourage you to try it, as well as the other bread and coffee cake recipes we served at the restaurant. You can make the dough into loaves instead of rolls, but I recommend a real oven instead of a metal box on the side of the road.

Grandma Ina and Grandpa Robert McCallum with Cindy, Mike, Pat, and Billy

Yeast likes a mildly warm temperature to rise; not too hot or too cool.

Good to Know

Don't add salt to the sponge; it will kill the yeast before it activates.

GRANDMA'S ROLLS

24 - 28 rolls

Sponge

1 1/2 cups 2% or whole milk, 100-110° F

1 tablespoon active dry yeast

1/2 cup granulated sugar

1 1/2 - 2 cups all-purpose flour

Dough

sponge (above)

1/4 cup vegetable oil or melted butter, cooled

2 eggs

2 teaspoons salt

3 - 3 1/2 cups all-purpose flour

1. Warm the milk on the stove or microwave until it is warm to the touch, just above body temperature, 100-110° F.
2. Place the yeast and sugar in a large mixing bowl or the bowl of a stand mixer.
3. Add the warmed milk and stir with a wire whisk until the yeast and sugar begin to dissolve.
4. Stir in the flour. The consistency should be similar to a thick cake batter. If it seems too thin, add a bit more flour.
5. Cover the bowl tightly with plastic wrap and allow it to sit in a warm area of the house for 30 to 40 minutes. It will rise and have a light, spongy consistency. .
6. Mix in the vegetable oil or melted butter, eggs, and salt using a wire whisk or the whisk attachment of a stand mixer.
7. Once the mixture is well combined, add 2 1/2 cups of flour. Use a wooden spoon to start incorporating the flour, then switch to using your hands to knead the dough or use the dough hook attachment of a stand mixer. Add more flour as you need it. The dough should form a ball and remain soft but not too sticky, or you won't be able to work with it.
8. Coat an extra-large bowl with cooking spray and place the ball of dough in it. Cover the bowl with a dish towel.
9. Allow the dough to rise in a warm area until it has doubled in size, approximately 2 hours.
10. Coat a sheet pan with cooking spray.
11. Turn the risen dough onto a lightly floured surface, punch the dough down, and form a rectangle. Cut into 6 strips.
12. Take each strip and cut 4 - 5 rolls, evenly sized. Place the rolls on the sheet pan about 2 inches apart. Allow the rolls to rise for another 30 to 40 minutes.
13. Preheat oven to 350° F.
14. Bake the risen rolls for 15 to 20 minutes or until golden brown.
15. Serve hot with butter.

For loaves: Divide the risen dough in half, shape into two loaves, and allow them to rise for 30 - 40 minutes in loaf pans. Bake for 35 - 40 minutes; the top should be browned and the loaf should sound hollow when tapped.

CINNAMON ROLLS

10 - 12 rolls

1 batch Grandma's Rolls dough (page 25)

1/3 cup butter, softened

1/2 cup granulated sugar

1/2 cup brown sugar

1 tablespoon cinnamon

*3/4 cup raisins, soaked (optional)

Glaze

1/4 cup butter, softened

1 1/2 cups powdered sugar

1 teaspoon vanilla extract

3 tablespoons milk

* Cover the raisins with hot tap water and allow them to soak for at least fifteen minutes. Drain and blot dry before adding them.

1. Make the dough according to instructions; it should be stickier than instructed for the dinner rolls.

2. Mix the sugar, brown sugar, and cinnamon in a small bowl.

3. Sprinkle flour over a large cutting board or countertop.

4. Once the dough has risen, turn it out onto the board. Rub some flour on your hands to help handle the sticky dough.

5. Gently pull the dough with your fingers or roll it out with a rolling pin until it is a large rectangle, approximately 18" x 12".

6. Using your fingers or a rubber spatula, spread the softened butter in a thin layer to cover the entire rectangle of dough.

7. Sprinkle the sugar and cinnamon mixture in a thin layer to cover the entire dough rectangle and follow with the raisins, if desired.

8. Begin rolling the dough from the bottom edge, using your fingers to stretch the dough and roll it over on itself.

9. Continue rolling until you reach the top. The dough should be sticky enough to stick to itself and close the roll, but if you need to "glue" it together, use a little softened butter.

10. Coat a large, rimmed sheet pan with butter or cooking spray.

11. Slice the dough roll into 10 - 12 pieces, each slice 1 1/2" to 2" thick.

12. Place the cinnamon rolls on the prepared sheet pan, about 2 1/2" apart. Allow the rolls to rise for 30 minutes before baking.

13. Preheat oven to 325° F.

14. Bake the cinnamon rolls for 25 to 35 minutes. They should be golden brown.

15. Mix the butter, powdered sugar, vanilla extract, and milk in a mixing bowl.

16. Spread or drizzle the glaze evenly over the cinnamon rolls.

Soft, sticky dough yields soft, delicious rolls

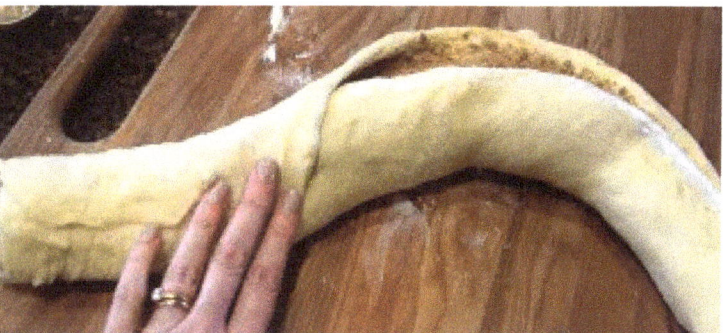

The coffee cake we offered alongside omelettes and continental breakfast at weekend brunch was a riff on a cake my mom often made for brothers Pat and Mike's birthdays.

Hers was called Sour Cream Walnut Cake, and she made it in a 9x13-inch Pyrex pan. It was not my favorite, but that is no reflection of the quality of the recipe. As a kid, I tended to react badly when presented with a non-chocolate dessert. I grew to love the version at the Treehouse, made in a bundt pan with pecans instead of walnuts.

SOUR CREAM & PECAN COFFEE CAKE

one bundt cake, 8 to 10 servings

1/2 cup butter, softened
1 cup granulated sugar
1 teaspoon vanilla
2 cups all-purpose flour
2 teaspoons baking powder
1 teaspoon baking soda
1/2 teaspoon salt
2 eggs
1 cup sour cream

Filling

1/2 cup brown sugar
1/4 cup granulated sugar
1 teaspoon cinnamon
1 tablespoon butter
1 tablespoon all-purpose flour
1 cup chopped pecans

Topping

2 tablespoons powdered sugar

1. Preheat oven to 350° F.
2. Generously coat a bundt pan with cooking spray.
3. Beat butter and sugar until light and fluffy. Add vanilla extract.
4. In a separate bowl, combine flour, baking powder, baking soda, and salt.
5. Add eggs, one at a time, to the butter mixture until well combined.
6. Add sour cream, then the flour mixture; mix until well combined after each addition.
7. In a separate bowl, combine all of the filling ingredients with a fork.
8. Spread half of the cake batter on the bottom of the prepared pan.
9. Sprinkle half of the filling mixture over the first layer of batter.
10. Repeat. The remaining filling mixture should be on top. Press it gently into the batter.
11. Bake for 40 to 50 minutes. A toothpick or sharp knife should come out clean when inserted in the center of the cake.
12. Allow the cake to cool in the bundt pan for at least 10 minutes before inverting it onto a cake plate or cardboard round.
13. Dust the coffee cake with sifted powdered sugar.
14. Serve warm or at room temperature.

BANANA BREAD

two 9 x 5-inch loaves

4 large bananas, very ripe
1 cup granulated sugar
1/2 cup vegetable oil or melted butter, cooled
2 eggs
1 teaspoon vanilla extract
2 cups all-purpose flour
1 teaspoon baking soda
1/2 teaspoon salt
1/2 teaspoon ground cinnamon
1/2 teaspoon ground nutmeg

1. Preheat oven to 350º F.
2. Coat two loaf pans with cooking spray.
3. Mash bananas with a wire whisk or masher in a large mixing bowl.
4. Add sugar and mix well with a wire whisk.
5. Add oil or butter, eggs, and vanilla extract; stir well after each addition.
6. In a separate large mixing bowl, stir to combine flour, baking soda, salt, cinnamon, and nutmeg.
7. Add the banana mixture to the dry mixture and stir until well combined.
8. Divide the batter evenly into the two prepared loaf pans.
9. Bake for 25 to 35 minutes. The top should be cracked, and a tester should come out clean when inserted in the center of the loaf. (Reduce baking time to 15 - 20 minutes for mini baking pans.)
10. Remove the bread from the pans and allow it to cool on a rack or cutting board for at least 15 minutes before slicing into it.
11. Cover or wrap and store at room temperature.

My daughter, Ella, mashing bananas while her sister, Hailey, waits her turn.

Mini loaf or bundt pans will also work well for this and the Date Nut Bread.

DATE NUT BREAD

two 9 x 5-inch loaves

11 ounces dried pitted dates, chopped (about 2 cups)

2 cups hot water

2 teaspoons baking soda

1/2 cup butter, softened

1 cup granulated sugar

1/2 cup brown sugar

2 eggs

1 tablespoon vanilla extract

1 1/2 teaspoons salt

4 cups all-purpose flour

1 1/2 cups roasted hazelnuts, chopped (page 56)

1. Preheat oven to 350º F.
2. Coat two loaf pans with cooking spray.
3. Chop the dates and place them in a large bowl with hot water and baking soda. Allow the dates to soak while you prepare the rest of the ingredients.
4. Place the butter, granulated sugar, and brown sugar in a large mixing bowl or the bowl of a stand mixer and beat until creamy.
5. Add eggs, one at a time, mixing well after each addition.
6. Add the vanilla and salt; mix well.
7. Slowly add the flour until well combined. The mixture will be dry and crumbly.
8. Add the soaked date mixture, do not drain as you want all the liquid, and slowly mix into the batter. Scrape the bottom and sides of the bowl to make sure the date mixture is thoroughly combined, and the batter is smooth.
9. Stir in the hazelnuts.
10. Divide the batter evenly into the two prepared loaf pans.
11. Bake for approximately one hour (reduce baking time to 25 - 30 minutes for mini baking pans). The top should be cracked, and the bread should be a dark golden brown. To test the middle, insert a sharp knife or toothpick; it should come out clean.
12. Remove from the pan and allow the bread to cool on a rack or cutting board for at least 15 minutes before slicing into it.
13. Cover or wrap and store at room temperature.

FOCACCIA

approximately 4 servings

1 cup warm water, 100-110° F

1 tablespoon active dry yeast

1/3 cup olive oil

1 1/4 teaspoon salt

1/2 teaspoon dried thyme

1/2 teaspoon dried oregano flakes

3 cups all-purpose or bread flour

Garlic Oil (Optional)

1 clove garlic, grated or finely chopped

1/4 teaspoon dried basil

1/4 teaspoon dried oregano flakes

1/4 teaspoon dried parsley flakes

1/4 teaspoon salt

freshly ground pepper and/or a few red pepper flakes

2 tablespoons olive oil

1. In a large mixing bowl or the bowl of a stand mixer, sprinkle the yeast over the warm water and allow it to sit for one minute.

2. Stir and add the olive oil, salt, thyme, and oregano. Whisk to combine.

3. Gradually add the flour, kneading with your hands or a stand mixer's dough hook until it forms a firm ball. It should be soft but not sticky.

4. Coat a large bowl with olive oil and transfer the dough to that bowl. Cover with a cloth and allow it to rise for 90 minutes. It should double in size.

5. Preheat oven to 475° F. If you have a pizza stone, preheat that too. If not, line a sheet pan with parchment paper and set it aside.

6. Toss the risen dough onto a lightly floured surface. Pressing gently with your fingers, flatten the dough into a 10" x 12" rectangle. Cut it in half.

Toppings

Here are some suggestions. Get creative and mix and match to your taste. Be careful not to weigh down the focaccia with too many toppings.

garlic oil (page 32)

pizza sauce (page 105)

pesto (page 89)

mozzarella

Parmesan

blue cheese/Gorgonzola

goat cheese

prosciutto

salami/pepperoni

caramelized onion (page 99)

roasted vegetables (red pepper, squash, cauliflower, etc.)

olives

tomatoes

fresh herbs

7. If you are putting additional toppings on the focaccia, pre-bake the dough for 10 -12 minutes or until it's light golden.

8. If you are using only the garlic oil, brush each half with the garlic oil before baking. Bake for 15 - 18 minutes or until golden brown.

9. Top pre-baked focaccia with your choice of sauce, cheese, meat, and/or vegetables, and bake for another 7 - 10 minutes.

10. Remove from the oven onto a cutting board. Cut into four triangles and serve hot.

Use a light touch with toppings!

Opposite page: Focaccia with garlic oil, ready to serve with soup or salad.
Top left: Focaccia with pizza sauce, mozzarella, and black olives.
Bottom right: Focaccia with garlic oil, caramelized onion, and Gorgonzola

CROUTONS

4 cups

4 cups crusty bread (French, sourdough, or Italian), cut into 1-inch cubes

1/4 cup olive oil

1/4 teaspoon salt

1/2 teaspoon dried thyme

1/4 teaspoon granulated garlic

1/4 teaspoon black pepper

1. Preheat oven to 375º F.
2. Place the cubed bread in a large bowl.
3. Mix the olive oil, salt, thyme, garlic, and black pepper in a smaller bowl.
4. Toss the oil mixture with the bread so it is well coated.
5. Spread the bread evenly on a sheet pan lined with parchment paper.
6. Bake for 10 - 15 minutes or until the croutons are golden brown.
7. Cool and store in an airtight container at room temperature.

Day-old bread works best

GARLIC CROSTINI

servings will vary

1/2 loaf French, Italian, or sourdough bread

1/4 cup olive oil

1 clove of garlic, grated

1/2 teaspoon dried basil

1/2 teaspoon dried oregano flakes

pinch of salt and black pepper

1/4 cup shredded Parmesan cheese

1. Thinly slice the bread, then cut each slice in half or quarters, depending on the size of the bread and how big or small you want the crostini.

2. Arrange the slices in a single layer on a sheet pan lined with parchment paper.

3. Mix the olive oil, grated garlic, basil, oregano, salt, and pepper in a small bowl.

4. Brush each slice of bread with the olive oil mixture, then top them with Parmesan cheese.

5. Place the oven rack close to the top and set the temperature to broil.

6. Broil the bread for 4 - 5 minutes. It should be sizzling and browned on the edges.

7. Serve it warm alongside Smoked Salmon Paté (page 115) or Hazelnut Pesto Dip (115).

EGGS & GRIDDLE

Eggs Benedict 40

Eggs Mornay 40

Omelette Fromage 42

Omelette Florentine 42

Omelette Piperade 42

Omelette Jambon 42

Omelette Champignon 42

Treehouse Quiche of the Day 44

Oven Baked Bacon 46

Bacon Bits 47

French Toast 48

Breakfast Potatoes 49

Bob's Pancakes 51

The casual elegance of a mid-morning brunch is ideal for special occasions and slow-paced weekend mornings.

Mother's Day was the busiest Sunday of the year at the Treehouse. Families brought mom in to enjoy Eggs Benedict, Omelettes, and Quiche of the Day served with fresh fruit and Cinnamon Rolls or Coffee Cake. Unlike many other restaurants offering lavish buffets, it was a seated affair with table service. Our mom, Betty, was not fond of buffets and insisted that standing in line dishing up one's own food did not enhance a dining experience, so a full menu was in order.

As wonderfully indulgent as it is to dine out for breakfast or brunch, there are significant benefits to preparing them at home, not least of which is staying in your slippers. Chef Billy has great tips for poaching eggs and building fantastic omelettes. You will find them in this chapter, along with his French Toast and Breakfast Potatoes recipes.

Also included in this chapter is my husband Bob's pancake recipe that his mom, Shirley, handed down to him. He made them for our daughters, Ella and Hailey, almost every weekend when they were little, and our neighbors often wandered over in search of them on a Saturday morning. They were perfect every time; fluffy with crisp edges, ready for butter and pure maple syrup. He often threw in a pan of Oven Baked Bacon to go along with them, and our girls learned how delicious it is to dip bacon into maple syrup.

Some of my best breakfast memories have come from sitting in the Treehouse dining room eating my favorite brunch entree, Omelette Champignon, and gathering at my parent's house after church for quiche and maple bars. Having pancakes with Bob and our girls on Saturday mornings in pj's remains the most priceless.

I hope you find a favorite combination of egg and griddle recipes to share with family and friends while you pause and enjoy a leisurely meal.

EGGS BENEDICT

2 servings

4 eggs

dash of salt

1 teaspoon white vinegar

2 English muffins

4 slices Canadian bacon or ham or 4 ounces smoked salmon

1 cup Hollandaise Sauce (page 85)

chopped parsley (optional)

1. Make the hollandaise sauce and keep it warm according to the recipe instructions.
2. Fill a medium-sized saucepan about halfway with water.
3. Bring the water to a boil, then turn down the heat so the water is barely simmering.
4. Break the muffins in half and toast in a toaster or on a flat-top grill.
5. Warm the Canadian bacon, ham, or smoked salmon in a sauté pan or on a flat-top grill.
6. Add salt and white vinegar to the water.
7. Gently drop the eggs, one at a time, into the simmering water.
8. Cook 2-3 minutes for soft yolks, 4 minutes for "jammy" yolks, or 5 minutes for hard yolks.
9. Top each muffin-half with Canadian bacon, ham, or smoked salmon, a poached egg, and hollandaise sauce.
10. Garnish with parsley and serve hot.

EGGS MORNAY

2 servings

4 eggs

dash of salt

1 teaspoon white vinegar

1 tablespoon butter or cooking oil

3 cups sliced mushrooms

1 cup prepared Swiss Cheese Mornay Sauce (page 87)

1/4 cup grated Swiss cheese

chopped parsley (optional)

1. Make the mornay sauce and keep it warm.
2. Fill a medium-sized saucepan about halfway with water.
3. Bring the water to a boil, then turn down the heat so the water is barely simmering.
4. Melt the butter or heat the cooking oil in a large sauté pan over medium-high heat.
5. Add the sliced mushrooms and sauté until they are browned and reduced to about half their original volume (1 1/2 cups).
6. Add salt and white vinegar to the water.
7. Gently drop the eggs, one at a time, into the simmering water.
8. Cook 2-3 minutes for soft yolks, 4 minutes for "jammy" yolks, or 5 minutes for hard yolks.
9. Arrange the mushrooms on two separate plates.
10. Top them with two poached eggs and mornay sauce.
11. Garnish with grated Swiss cheese and parsley, and serve hot.

Poaching Tips

* Use fresh eggs and add white vinegar for firm whites.

* Bring the water to a boil, then turn down the heat, so it's at a low simmer before you drop the eggs in; boiling will cause them to scramble.

* Crack each egg into a small bowl before gently dropping it in the water to ensure the yolk is intact.

* Don't crowd the eggs in the pan. Work in batches if necessary.

* Be patient and allow the eggs to simmer for at least two minutes before attempting to move them.

* Use a slotted spoon to remove the eggs and blot them on a clean towel before serving.

TREEHOUSE OMELETTES

each variation makes one large omelette

Base

3 large eggs

pinch of salt

white or black pepper

1 tablespoon butter or canola oil

Omelette Fromage

3/4 cup grated cheddar and/or Swiss cheese

Omelette Fromage

Omelette Florentine

3 cups fresh spinach, chopped and lightly sautéed (it will shrink to about 1/3 cup)

1/2 cup grated Swiss cheese

Omelette Piperade

1/2 cup diced red bell pepper (any color), sautéed

1/4 cup chopped onion, sautéed

5 grape tomatoes, halved and sautéed

1/2 cup grated cheddar cheese

Omelette Florentine with Breakfast Potatoes (page 49)

Omelette Jambon

1/3 cup diced ham

1/2 cup grated cheddar cheese

Omelette Piperade

Omelette Champignon

1 1/2 cups sliced fresh mushrooms, sautéed

1/4 cup bacon bits (page 47)

1/4 cup Hollandaise Sauce (page 85)

Omelette Champignon

Omelette Prep & Assembly

1. Make the hollandaise sauce for Omelette Champignon, if necessary.
2. Prep the ingredients for your filling so they are ready to use. Grate or crumble cheeses and chop and cook meats and vegetables as necessary.
3. Whisk eggs, salt, and pepper in a mixing bowl until thoroughly combined.
4. Melt/heat 1 tablespoon butter or cooking oil in an 8-inch nonstick sauté pan over medium heat.
5. Pour in the eggs.
6. Once they start to cook, tilt the pan and use a rubber spatula to gently lift underneath the eggs, allowing the raw egg to run off. Repeat this around the pan's edges until most of the egg is cooked.
7. Flip to cook the remaining raw egg.
8. For open-faced Omelette Piperade: Top the cooked eggs with the sautéed peppers, onion, and tomatoes. Sprinkle with grated cheddar and place under the oven broiler to melt the cheese; about 3 - 5 minutes.
9. For folded omelettes: Immediately add the fillings and gently fold the omelette in half using the rubber spatula.
10. Allow cheese to melt inside the omelette; briefly cover the pan if necessary.
11. Transfer the omelette to a plate and serve.

43

TREEHOUSE QUICHE OF THE DAY

8 servings

one 9-inch pie crust, raw or parbaked
(try Rich Butter Pie Crust page 242)

5 eggs

3/4 cup heavy cream

3/4 cup whole milk

1/2 teaspoon salt

1/4 teaspoon black or white pepper

1/4 teaspoon granulated garlic

1 - 1 1/2 cups grated or shredded cheese
(options below)

SMOKED SALMON

1 cup shredded mozzarella cheese

4 ounces cream cheese, chunked

4 ounces smoked salmon

2 tablespoons fresh dill or 2 teaspoons dried dill

SPINACH, SWISS, AND FETA

1 cup shredded Swiss or Jarlsberg cheese

1/3 cup crumbled feta

3 cups baby spinach, chopped

HAM AND CHEDDAR

1 1/2 cups shredded cheddar cheese

6 ounces ham, chopped

2 tablespoons chopped green onions or chives

BACON, GRUYÈRE, AND ONION

1 cup shredded gruyère cheese

4 ounces bacon bits, cooked (page 47)

1 cup caramelized onions (page 99)

VEGGIE

1 cup shredded Swiss or mozzarella cheese

1/4 cup grated Parmesan cheese

1 cup baby spinach, chopped

1/2 cup broccoli, chopped and blanched

1/2 cup sautéed sliced mushrooms

1/2 cup sautéed bell peppers

8 - 10 grape tomatoes, halved

1 tablespoon fresh basil

1. Prepare the crust.
2. Preheat oven to 350º F.
3. Grate or crumble cheeses and chop and cook meats and vegetables as necessary.
4. Whisk together the eggs, cream, milk, salt, pepper, granulated garlic, and any dried herbs you might use in a large mixing bowl. Set aside.
5. Spread shredded cheese on the bottom of the crust.
6. Follow with additional cheese crumbles or chunks (feta, cream cheese, etc.).
7. Add proteins, veggies, and fresh herbs, spreading each in an even layer.
8. Give the egg mixture a good stir, then slowly pour the mixture into the pie shell. It should come up to the top of the fillings.
9. Gently press down any fillings not covered before baking.
10. Cover the exposed edges of the crust with aluminum foil. Bake for 50 to 60 minutes. The center should be risen and feel firm when pressed.
11. Allow the quiche to cool for at least 15 minutes before cutting and serving.

Get creative!
Mix and match ingredients as you like.

OVEN BAKED BACON

6 - 8 servings

2 pounds thick-cut bacon

1. Preheat oven to 400º F.

2. Line a rimmed 12" x 18" sheet pan with heavy-duty aluminum foil or parchment paper. Place a stainless steel rack on top if you have one.

3. Place individual slices of bacon side by side on the rack or directly on the foil or parchment paper. The slices can touch each other to fit more on the pan.

4. Bake in preheated oven for 20 - 30 minutes, depending on the bacon's thickness. Check the bacon often and turn the slices after 12 to 15 minutes. Use care when handling the pan, as there will be hot bacon grease that could spill out.

5. Line a large plate or platter with a paper towel.

6. Remove the cooked bacon from the oven and immediately transfer it to the paper towel-lined plate/platter to drain off the grease.

7. Serve hot bacon immediately or keep it warm in the oven, in foil or a covered pan, at 200º F.

BACON BITS

serving size will vary depending on use

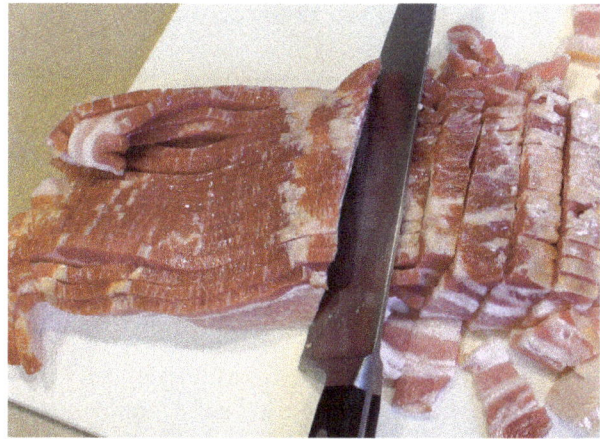

2 pounds thick-cut bacon

1. Cut bacon strips into pieces, 1/2 to 1-inch cuts, depending on the size you want. Keep in mind they will shrink in size.

2. Place the bacon in a high-sided heavy skillet or Dutch oven.

3. Cook on medium to medium-high heat, stirring occasionally.

4. If the bacon has previously been frozen, there will be excess liquid that needs to drain. Use a large spoon to drain it off as you cook it, so the bacon fat can render properly.

5. Once the fat renders and browns the bacon, keep a close eye on it and cook to desired doneness and crispness.

6. Place a strainer over a heatproof bowl, then transfer the bacon into the strainer to drain the fat.

7. Refrigerate and use within 5 days.

Use in omelettes, quiche, salads, and soups

FRENCH TOAST

2 - 3 servings

*4 – 6 thick slices of white bread

3 eggs

1/2 teaspoon cinnamon

1/4 teaspoon pure vanilla extract

pinch of salt

1/2 cup half & half (sub with 2% or whole milk if you don't have it on hand)

1/2 cup 2% or whole milk

butter for the griddle

pure maple syrup

fresh berries

powdered sugar

* We baked Grandma's Roll dough (page 25) into loaves at the Treehouse, but any thick-cut white bread will work. Day-old bread works best.

1. Preheat a griddle or skillet on medium heat.
2. Whisk together eggs, cinnamon, vanilla, and salt in a large mixing bowl.
3. Pour in the half & half and milk; stir until well combined.
4. Dip the bread, no more than two pieces at a time, into the custard mixture, soaking it thoroughly.
5. Working quickly, spread the butter on the griddle to coat it. (I like to leave it on the butter knife to spread it on the griddle, or you can use a spatula.) It should sizzle, but it shouldn't burn and smoke, so adjust the stove's temperature before placing the soaked bread on the griddle.
6. Cook the French toast for about 3 minutes on each side. The outside should be golden brown, and the inside should expand and be firm to the touch once the custard is cooked through.
7. Serve hot with your favorite accompaniments. I like my French toast with fresh strawberries.

Chef Billy hates strawberries; he's weird that way. A little sprinkle of powdered sugar and pure maple syrup are really all you need.

BREAKFAST POTATOES

3 - 4 servings

6 – 8 small red and/or white potatoes

salt

seasoned salt (store–bought or your own favorite seasonings)

vegetable/canola oil

1. Place potatoes in a large pot. Fill with water until it comes up about two inches above the potatoes.

2. Add a couple good pinches of salt and bring the water and potatoes to a rolling boil over medium-high heat.

3. Reduce the heat to low and simmer for about 20 minutes. The potatoes should be tender when pierced with a fork.

4. Allow the potatoes to cool slightly, then slice them into rounds, approximately 1/2-inch thick.

5. Sprinkle the sliced potatoes with seasoned salt.

6. Preheat a griddle or skillet (I like to use cast iron, we had a big flat-top grille at the restaurant) over medium-high heat.

Boil potatoes for dinner the night before to save time in the morning

7. Generously coat the preheated griddle/skillet with oil.

8. Place each slice of potato down on the oiled griddle/skillet.

9. Cook for about 5 minutes, then turn and cook the other side until both sides are nicely browned.

10. Serve hot alongside your favorite breakfast entrée.

BOB'S PANCAKES

15 - 20 pancakes

3 eggs
2 cups milk
1/3 cup vegetable oil
2 3/4 cups flour
1/4 cup granulated sugar
3/4 teaspoon salt
1 tablespoon baking powder

butter or vegetable oil

1. Preheat the oven to 200º F in case you need to keep the pancakes warm.

2. Beat the eggs in a large bowl. Add the milk and oil and mix well.

3. In a separate bowl, stir together the flour, sugar, salt, and baking powder until they are well combined.

4. Add the flour mixture to the egg mixture and stir to combine. Do not overmix; there may be some lumps. Let the batter rest while you heat up the griddle.

5. Preheat a stovetop griddle, electric griddle, or large, heavy skillet over medium heat.

6. Test the heat by tossing a drop of water on the pan; if it sizzles, it's ready to cook the pancakes.

7. Coat the surface of the griddle or skillet with a thin layer of butter or oil.

8. Drop batter, about 1/4 cup at a time, into circles on the griddle, leaving space between each.

9. Cook for 1 - 2 minutes until the surface of the pancake bubbles and the cooked side is golden brown. Flip and cook another 1 - 2 minutes.

10. Keep the pancakes warm in the oven then serve them with butter, syrup, and Oven-Baked Bacon (page 46).

SALAD & DRESSINGS

Oregon Fruit & Hazelnut Salad 57

Treehouse Caesar Salad 58

Hot Spinach and Shrimp 59

Oregon Bay Shrimp Louie 60

Acapulco Almond Salad 61

French Style Potato Salad 62

Mom's Potato Salad 63

House Vinaigrette 64

Sweet & Sour 64

Thousand Island Dressing 64

Basic Balsamic Vinaigrette 64

Poppyseed Dressing 65

Buttermilk Blue Cheese Dressing 65

Caesar Dressing 65

Mexican Orange Dressing 65

I recently remarked to a friend how surprised I was as an adult to learn that people came from all over the world to visit the Oregon Coast and the greater Pacific Northwest.

Growing up in Eugene, I took for granted the mere hour it took to get to Florence's ocean beaches and dunes. I never thought twice about the few hours it took to reach our favorite camping spot in the Cascade mountains or the abundance of green rolling hills rich with hazelnut orchards, vineyards, and some of the finest produce you will ever find in the Willamette Valley right outside our door.

As it often does for those of us who grew up in extraordinary parts of the world, it took moving two thousand miles away for me to appreciate the gifts of the place I was born. Twenty-five years ago, my husband Bob and I were thrilled to move to the Chicago area, where they are rightfully known for their great food. We quickly learned, however, that while we were eating some of the best steak and pizza of our lives, we missed the abundance of produce we were accustomed to back home. We also missed the mountains and the ocean more than I thought possible. Fortunately, we had Lake Michigan and the city to explore and enjoy until we returned to Oregon a decade later. I still miss Gino's East deep-dish pizza, but the fresh Dungeness crab from the Pacific Ocean and berries, hazelnuts, pears, and apples from the Willamette and Hood River valleys more than make up for it.

I've included my favorite salad in this chapter. The Oregon Fruit and Hazelnut Salad was not on the Treehouse menu, but I think it should have been. The combination of seasonal fruit, blue cheese, greens, and toasted hazelnuts is something I could eat every day. I make it with summer berries, peaches, pears, apples, or whatever I have on hand. Basic Balsamic Vinaigrette perfectly accentuates the fruit and cheese flavors or try it with Poppyseed Dressing as shown on the opposite page.

Mom's parents,
Grandpa Tom and Grandma Ilah Martin,
on their farm in Silverton, Oregon

You won't want to miss Chef Billy's unique caesar salad preparation.

He's perfected our dad's recipe. Not only did he serve it for years at the Treehouse, Billy Mac's, and McCallum's Custom Catering, but it is always on our table at Christmas dinner to accompany the Whiskey Cured Prime Rib. The dressing is a little lighter and less creamy in texture than you might be used to, but the flavor is bold and lemony with a kick of heat and plenty of garlic. Add blackened or grilled salmon, steak, or chicken to take it from a side salad to an entrée.

If you are fortunate enough to live in the Pacific Northwest, take a moment to appreciate what surrounds you. Pick up some Dungeness crab and bay shrimp to make a delicious Louie salad, and purchase sweet fruit and fresh vegetables from a local farmstand. Maybe even stop in at a local winery for a crisp Sauvignon Blanc or Pinot Gris to accompany the salads you'll find in this chapter.

Wherever you live, remember or find out what makes your region extraordinary and enjoy your local harvest.

Roast and Skin Hazelnuts

* Preheat oven to 350º F.
* Shell hazelnuts (if necessary) and place raw hazelnuts on a rimmed baking pan.
* Roast for 15 - 20 minutes. The hazelnut skins should be blistered, and the inside golden brown.
* Remove them from the oven, and immediately, while they are still hot, place the hazelnuts on a large dish towel.
* Wrap them up in the towel, twisting the top, and allow them to steam for a few minutes.
* Massage the hazelnuts in the towel to remove the skins. They don't always come off completely.
* Pick out the hazelnuts and discard the skins.

Use in these recipes

* Chocolate Chunk Brownies (page 206)
* Date Nut Bread (page 31)
* Hazelnut Pesto (page 89)
* Hazelnut Pesto Dip (page 115)
* Oregon Fruit & Hazelnut Salad (page 57)
* Hazelnut Cheesecake (page 228)

OREGON FRUIT & HAZELNUT SALAD

2 large or 4 small salads

1 head of romaine lettuce, chopped (about 6 cups)

1 fresh apple, pear, and/or peach; sliced

1 cup fresh berries (raspberries, blackberries, blueberries, etc.)

1/2 cup chopped roasted hazelnuts

1/2 cup crumbled blue cheese

Basic Balsamic Vinaigrette (page 64) or Poppyseed Dressing (page 65)

Arrange ingredients artfully on a large platter or individual plates.

CHEF BILLY'S CAESAR SALAD

2 large or 4 small salads

1 head of romaine lettuce, chopped (about 6 cups)

1 cup Croutons (page 34)

1/3 cup shredded Parmesan cheese

1/3 cup Caesar Dressing (page 65)

OPTIONAL

8 – 12 ounces of grilled steak, chicken, or salmon

6 – 8 ounces of cooked crab or bay shrimp

lemon wedges

1. Toss the lettuce, croutons, Parmesan, and caesar dressing in a large bowl.
2. Serve on salad plates with lemon wedges.
3. Top individual salads with steak, chicken, salmon, crab, or shrimp if desired.

HOT SPINACH & SHRIMP

2 large or 4 small salads

6 cups baby spinach (loosely packed)

12 – 16 jumbo shrimp, peeled and deveined (see tips, page 154)

1 tablespoon canola oil

1/3 cup bacon bits (page 47)

6 ounces Sweet & Sour (page 64)

sesame seeds

lemon wedges

your choice of fresh fruit and vegetables (berries, oranges, grapes, tomatoes, cucumbers, onion, bell peppers, etc.)

1. Divide spinach among two large plates.
2. Preheat canola oil in a large sauté pan over medium-high heat until hot, but not smoking.
3. Add shrimp and sauté until pink and cooked through, 1 - 2 minutes per side.
4. Add the bacon bits and Sweet & Sour to the shrimp. Bring the dressing to a boil and toss it with the prawns and bacon in the sauté pan.
5. Remove the shrimp with tongs and arrange them on top of the spinach.
6. Pour the hot dressing and bacon over the shrimp and spinach.
7. Sprinkle with sesame seeds and garnish with lemon wedges and your choice of fresh fruit and vegetables.

OREGON BAY SHRIMP LOUIE

2 large or 4 small salads

1 head of romaine lettuce, chopped (about 6 cups)

8 ounces cooked bay shrimp (aka baby shrimp)

2 hard-boiled eggs, sliced

your choice of sliced vegetables (carrot, bell pepper, avocado, cucumber, tomato, etc.)

12 black olives, halved

lemon wedges

Thousand Island Dressing (page 64)

1. Lay a bed of lettuce down on each plate.
2. Place the shrimp on top of the lettuce, making a mound in the center.
3. Arrange the sliced eggs, vegetables, olives, and lemon wedges around the shrimp.
4. Serve with Thousand Island Dressing.

Also great with Dungeness crab!

ACAPULCO ALMOND SALAD

2 large or 4 small salads

12 ounces baked or grilled marinated chicken breast, cold (page 91)

1 head of romaine lettuce, chopped (about 6 cups)

1 small zucchini, chopped

1 cucumber, sliced

1 – 2 oranges, peeled and sliced

fresh berries, melon, pineapple, and/or grapes

about 8 thin slices of red onion

1 cup slivered or chopped toasted almonds

Mexican Orange Dressing (page 65)

1. Slice the cooked chicken breast into strips.
2. Arrange romaine lettuce in an even layer on a dinner plate.
3. Arrange the chicken, vegetables, and fruit into decorative segments atop the lettuce.
4. Before serving, garnish with the toasted almonds and dress with Mexican Orange Dressing.
5. Serve with sliced Date Nut Bread (page 31) or Banana Bread (page 30) for the complete Treehouse experience.

Perfect for a summer lunch or brunch with friends

FRENCH STYLE POTATO SALAD

8 - 10 servings

3 pounds baby red potatoes

a couple pinches of salt

1/2 red onion, finely chopped (about 1/2 cup)

4 ribs of celery, finely chopped (about 1 cup)

1 bunch of flat-leaf parsley, finely chopped (about 1/3 cup)

1/2 cup dill relish or 1/2 cup dill pickle, finely chopped

3/4 cup House Vinaigrette Dressing (page 64)

1/4 cup Dijon mustard

1/2 teaspoon minced or grated fresh garlic

1 teaspoon Worcestershire sauce

1/4 - 1/2 teaspoon salt

1/4 - 1/2 teaspoon black pepper

1. Place potatoes in a large pot. Fill with water until it comes up about two inches above the potatoes.

2. Bring to a boil over medium-high heat, throw in a couple good pinches of salt, cover, and continue to boil for 20 - 25 minutes or until tender. Adjust heat to prevent the water from boiling over. To test for doneness, a fork should easily pierce an individual potato.

3. While the potatoes are cooking, prep the rest of the ingredients.

4. Place the chopped onion, celery, parsley, and dill relish in a large mixing bowl.

5. Whisk the vinaigrette with the Dijon mustard, minced garlic, and Worcestershire sauce in a separate bowl.

6. Drain the cooked potatoes and allow them to cool for ten minutes or so.

7. Cut the warm potatoes in halves or quarters and add them to the vegetables in the large bowl.

8. Pour the vinaigrette over the potatoes and vegetables and gently stir until the dressing is fully distributed.

9. Add salt and pepper to your taste and give the salad a good stir before refrigerating.

10. You can serve the salad right away, but it's best to allow it to chill for at least 2 hours.

MOM'S POTATO SALAD

8 - 10 servings

3 pounds of Yukon gold potatoes

salt

4 eggs, hard-boiled

1/2 large onion, chopped (about 1 1/2 cups)

1 cup celery, chopped

1/2 cup bread & butter pickles, chopped

Dressing

1 3/4 cups mayonnaise

juice of 1/2 lemon

2 tablespoons bread and butter pickle juice

2 tablespoons mustard (Dijon, stoneground, or horseradish)

1/2 teaspoon salt

1 teaspoon smoked paprika

1 teaspoon dried dill

1/2 teaspoon dried thyme

dash of cayenne pepper or hot sauce

Garnish

Fresh herbs, chopped fine, to add color and freshness (parsley, thyme, chives, and dill are all good choices)

smoked paprika

1. Peel and quarter the potatoes and put them in a large pot. Fill with water until it comes up about two inches above the potatoes.
2. Bring to a boil over medium-high heat, throw in a couple good pinches of salt, and continue to boil for 15 - 20 minutes. Adjust the heat down to prevent the water from boiling over.
3. Place the four eggs into a saucepan and cover them with about an inch of cold water.
4. Bring the eggs to a boil over high heat, then turn the heat down to medium, and allow them to simmer for about 12 minutes (for a medium-sized egg). Submerge the cooked eggs in cold water to cool before peeling and chopping.
5. While the potatoes and eggs cook, chop the onion, celery, and pickles.
6. Combine all of the ingredients for the dressing in a mixing bowl.
7. Test the potatoes for doneness. They should be tender enough for a fork to pierce through the center easily. Drain them, then cut them into bite-size pieces.
8. Combine the warm potatoes with the eggs, onion, celery, pickles, and dressing in a large bowl. Remember, the dressing will soak into the potatoes as the salad chills, so be generous with it.
9. Taste the salad and add more salt and pepper as needed.
10. Chill the salad for at least a couple of hours before serving.
11. Garnish with fresh herbs and paprika.

HOUSE VINAIGRETTE

approximately 1 1/2 cups

1/2 cup olive oil

1/2 cup canola oil

1/3 cup white wine vinegar

2 tablespoons lemon juice

1/2 teaspoon salt

1/2 teaspoon black pepper

1/4 teaspoon dried tarragon

1/4 teaspoon ground sage

1/4 teaspoon dry mustard (or 1/2 teaspoon prepared, such as Dijon)

Briskly whisk or blend all ingredients. Mix in 1/4 cup of blue cheese, feta, or gorgonzola if desired. Dress your favorite green salad.

Store in the refrigerator for up to two weeks.

SWEET & SOUR

approximately 1 1/3 cups

1/3 cup granulated sugar

1/3 cup white vinegar

2/3 cup vegetable/canola oil

Whisk all ingredients together until the sugar is dissolved.

Store in the refrigerator for up to two weeks.

THOUSAND ISLAND DRESSING

approximately 4 cups

3 cups mayonnaise

1/4 cup sour cream

1/3 cup Sweet & Sour (this page)

1/3 cup tomato paste

1/4 cup dill relish

1/2 teaspoon granulated garlic

1 1/2 teaspoons salt

3/4 teaspoon black pepper

3/4 teaspoon Worcestershire sauce

1/2 cup buttermilk or milk

Stir together all ingredients. Add more milk or buttermilk for desired consistency.

Store in the refrigerator for 3 to 5 days.

BASIC BALSAMIC VINAIGRETTE

approximately 3/4 cup

1/4 cup balsamic vinegar

1/2 cup olive oil

1 small or 1/2 large clove garlic, grated

1/8 teaspoon salt

1/8 teaspoon black pepper

Briskly whisk or blend all ingredients.

Store in the refrigerator for up to two weeks.

POPPYSEED DRESSING

approximately 1 cup

1 cup Sweet & Sour (page 64)

1/4 cup poppy seeds

1/4 teaspoon granulated garlic

Combine ingredients; stir before each use. Store in the refrigerator for up to two weeks.

BUTTERMILK BLUE CHEESE DRESSING

approximately 3 cups

2 cups mayonnaise

1/2 cup sour cream

2 ounces blue cheese crumbles

1 teaspoon lemon juice

1/2 teaspoon white wine vinegar

1/2 teaspoon salt

1/2 teaspoon black pepper

1/4 teaspoon granulated garlic

dash of Worcestershire sauce

1/3 to 1/2 cup buttermilk

Stir together all of the ingredients. Begin with 1/3 cup of the buttermilk and add more for desired consistency.

Store in the refrigerator for 3 to 5 days.

CAESAR DRESSING

approximately 1 1/4 cups

2 tablespoons chopped garlic

2 teaspoons red wine vinegar

2 tablespoons lemon juice

4 shakes Tobasco sauce

1 teaspoon dry mustard

1 1/4 teaspoons Worcestershire sauce

1/8 teaspoon salt

1/8 teaspoon white pepper

1/2 cup olive oil

1/2 cup canola oil

Place all ingredients in a food processor or blender and blend until the dressing is well combined and thickened.

Store in the refrigerator for up to two weeks.

MEXICAN ORANGE DRESSING

approximately 1 3/4 cups

3 ounces frozen orange juice concentrate, melted

1/4 cup honey

1/2 cup white wine vinegar

1/4 teaspoon cayenne pepper

1/4 teaspoon salt

1 cup vegetable or canola oil

Whisk together the orange juice concentrate, honey, vinegar, cayenne, and salt. Slowly but vigorously, whisk in the oil until the dressing is well combined and thickened.

Store in the refrigerator for up to one week.

SOUP DU JOUR

Tillamook Cheddar Cheese Soup 70

Cream of Potato Soup 71

Chicken with Wild Rice Soup 72

French Onion Soup 73

Gazpacho 74

Italian Vegetable Soup 75

Clam Chowder 76

Cream of Mushroom Soup 79

To me, soup is the ultimate comfort food.

Not only is it delicious and nourishing, it's also quite satisfying to prepare. I enjoy the process of making the roux, chopping the vegetables, selecting the spices, and bringing all the ingredients together with a fragrant broth. In the cool days of autumn and winter, soup is often the center of cozy family evenings in our home.

At the Treehouse, a double burner with large pots of soup was conveniently located where the waitstaff could ladle steaming bowls without involving the cooks. That easy access and the promise of no charge meant many employees practically lived on dipping Grandma's Rolls into Tillamook Cheddar Cheese Soup or the daily soup offering between shifts.

This is one example of how the restaurant became like a second home for staff members. Many attended the University of Oregon or Northwest Christian College and were away from family. My parents and older siblings made them feel like they were part of our family by feeding them, counseling them, inviting them on family camping trips, and bringing them home if they had no place to go for holidays. After long shifts, they would sit in the downstairs bar with a group of staff members until the wee hours of the morning, drinking wine and "solving the world's problems."

Today, we may view that relationship between management and employees as a cautionary tale rather than a good example, but it was a different time. The employees felt nurtured and cared for, which was important and came naturally to my family. Long after the working relationship was over, strong bonds remained.

Cream of Mushroom Soup

Chicken with Wild Rice Soup

The soups in this chapter were featured at the Treehouse as "Soup du Jour" offerings. My favorites are the Italian Vegetable and Chicken with Wild Rice. As a kid, I would help myself to a bowl or two as I sat in the downstairs office behind the bar, doing homework and waiting for my mom to finish up for the night.

If I was lucky, I could overhear the after-hours conversations and learn the solutions to all the world's problems.

TILLAMOOK CHEDDAR CHEESE SOUP

4 - 6 servings

2 tablespoons butter

1/4 cup all-purpose flour

3/4 teaspoons salt

1/4 teaspoon white pepper

1/4 teaspoon ground or grated nutmeg

1/8 teaspoon granulated garlic

2 1/2 cups water

1/4 cup heavy cream

10 ounces Tillamook cheddar cheese, grated

1 teaspoon lemon juice

4 dashes of hot sauce

apple slices (for garnish)

1. Combine butter, flour, salt, pepper, nutmeg, and granulated garlic in a medium-sized saucepan.
2. Stir over medium-low heat until the butter has melted and the ingredients are well combined into a thick roux.
3. Add water one-half cup at a time with a wire whisk. Stir well after each addition to ensure a smooth texture.
4. Once all the water has been added, increase heat to medium-high and, stirring constantly, bring to a boil.
5. Boil and continue to stir for two to three minutes. It should be thick enough to coat the back of a spoon when tested.
6. Stir in the heavy cream.
7. Add the grated cheddar and stir until smooth.
8. Add lemon juice and hot sauce.
9. Serve immediately, or use a double boiler to keep the soup warm without scorching the bottom of the pan.
10. Garnish with apple slices and serve with Grandma's Rolls. (page 25)

Roux: a mixture of flour and fat used as a thickening agent in a soup or sauce

CREAM OF POTATO SOUP

10 -12 servings

2 tablespoons olive oil

1 yellow onion, peeled and chopped

4 ribs of celery, chopped

1 teaspoon ground rosemary

1 teaspoon dried thyme

2 teaspoons dried parsley

1/2 teaspoon white pepper

1 teaspoon salt

2 pounds red or white potatoes

2 cloves garlic, peeled and chopped

4 ounces (about 1 cup) bacon bits (page 47)

1 bay leaf

1 quart of chicken or vegetable stock

3 tablespoons butter

3 tablespoons flour

1/2 cup heavy cream

freshly ground black pepper

Garnish

sour cream or Greek yogurt

chopped parsley or chives

1. Chop the onion and celery into approximately 1/2-inch dice and place in a large stock pot or Dutch oven with the olive oil.
2. Turn the heat to medium, and add the rosemary, thyme, parsley, white pepper, and salt.
3. Sauté, stirring occasionally, until the onions and celery begin to soften.
4. Meanwhile, chop the potatoes into approximately 1-inch chunks.
5. Add the potatoes, garlic, and bacon to the pot and sauté, stirring often, for about 5 minutes.
6. Add the bay leaf and pour in the chicken or vegetable stock.
7. Bring the soup to a low boil over medium-high heat, then turn the heat to low and allow it to simmer for 20 - 30 minutes. The potatoes should be tender when pierced with a fork before proceeding to the next step.
8. Melt the butter in the microwave or over the stove. Whisk in the flour until the mixture is a smooth roux.
9. Stir the roux into the hot soup until it is thoroughly combined. Increase the heat to medium-high and allow it to cook and thicken for about 5 minutes, stirring often.
10. Garnish with sour cream and parsley or chives before serving.

CHICKEN WITH WILD RICE SOUP

6 - 8 servings

5 cups chicken stock or broth, divided

1/3 cup wild rice (or long grain white rice)

1 – 2 tablespoons olive oil

12 ounces chicken breast, diced (raw or cooked)

1 cup chopped yellow onion

1 cup chopped celery

1/2 teaspoon salt

1/2 teaspoon white pepper

2 teaspoons dried dill weed

1 teaspoon dried basil

1/2 teaspoon ground sage

1/4 teaspoon ground rosemary

1 bay leaf

8 ounces sliced mushrooms

2 – 4 cloves garlic, peeled and minced

1/4 cup white wine

1 tablespoon lemon juice

3 tablespoons butter

3 tablespoons all-purpose flour

1/4 cup tomato paste

1/2 cup heavy cream

Garnish

sour cream

fresh dill

1. Bring 4 cups of the chicken stock or broth to a boil in a medium-sized saucepan. Add rice and simmer for 30 minutes. (This should be adequate time to complete the following steps. If not, simply remove the pan from the heat until you are ready to use the stock and rice in the soup.)

2. Meanwhile, coat the bottom of a large stock pot or Dutch oven with olive oil.

3. Add raw chicken and sauté, stirring often on medium-high heat, until fully cooked. (If your chicken is already cooked, you may skip this step.) Remove the chicken from the pot and set aside.

4. Add the chopped onion and celery to the pot; add a bit more olive oil, if necessary. Sauté over medium heat with the salt, white pepper, dill, basil, sage, rosemary, and bay leaf for about 5 minutes.

5. Add the mushrooms, garlic, and chicken. Sauté for another few minutes.

6. Add the white wine and lemon juice and allow the wine to simmer and reduce for about 5 minutes.

7. Stir in the chicken stock and rice and set the heat to simmer.

8. Using the pan you just emptied of stock and rice, melt the butter and flour together to make a roux. Cook over medium heat for 2 - 3 minutes until golden in color.

9. Slowly stir the remaining one cup of chicken stock into the roux with a wire whisk, stirring constantly until smooth.

10. Whisk the thickened stock into the soup and stir well to avoid lumps. Add the tomato paste, then the heavy cream, and allow the soup to cook over medium heat until it thickens, about 10 minutes.

11. Keep the soup warm until you are ready to serve. Garnish with sour cream and dill.

Pictured on page 69

FRENCH ONION SOUP

4 servings

3 large sweet onions, peeled and sliced

1/4 cup butter

2 cloves garlic, peeled and thinly sliced

1/2 teaspoon salt

1/4 teaspoon black pepper

1 teaspoon dried thyme or 2 fresh thyme sprigs

1/3 cup red wine

4 cups beef stock or broth

Topping

1 1/2 cup croutons or 4 slices crostini (pages 34 and 35)

1 1/3 cups grated Swiss or Gruyère cheese

Garnish

fresh thyme

1. Peel and slice the onions into thin rings.
2. Melt the butter over medium heat in a large stockpot or Dutch oven.
3. Add the sliced onions, garlic, salt, black pepper, and dried thyme to the melted butter. Sauté over medium heat until the onions are soft and begin to caramelize. This should take about 20 minutes; you don't want the onions to brown too quickly.
4. Add the red wine and increase the heat to medium-high. Bring the wine to a boil. Reduce the heat to medium and cook for 3 - 5 minutes, stirring often, until the wine has reduced.
5. Stir in the beef stock/broth and simmer for 20 minutes. Keep the soup warm until you are ready to serve it.
6. Place four oven-safe bowls or ramekins on a cookie sheet.
7. Preheat oven to broil setting.
8. Fill the bowls or ramekins about 3/4 of the way with soup. (You may have soup left over).
9. Arrange the croutons or toasted bread to cover the top of each bowl of soup.
10. Sprinkle the grated cheese in a thick layer over the croutons or toasted bread.
11. Place the cookie sheet with the soup bowls on the top rack of your oven and broil for about 4 minutes until the cheese melts and begins to brown.
12. Garnish with a few leaves of fresh thyme and serve immediately.

GAZPACHO

12 - 14 servings

4 ribs of celery

1 medium yellow onion, peeled

1 bell pepper, cored, seeded

2 medium carrots, peeled

1 medium zucchini

1 medium yellow squash

12 large Roma tomatoes or 36 grape tomatoes

3 – 5 cloves of garlic, peeled

1 teaspoon dried tarragon or 1 tablespoon fresh tarragon

1 teaspoon dried basil or 1 tablespoon fresh basil

1 teaspoon dried oregano or 1 tablespoon fresh oregano

6 cups low-sodium tomato juice

1 cup red wine vinegar

1/2 cup lemon juice

1/4 cup olive oil

6 dashes hot sauce

1 teaspoon salt

1/2 teaspoon black pepper

Garnish

radish/chives/green onion

1. Prepare the vegetables by cleaning, trimming the ends, and peeling them as necessary.

2. Chop celery, onion, bell pepper, carrots, zucchini, yellow squash, and tomatoes in about 1/4 inch dice.

3. Place in a large bowl.

4. Grate or mince the garlic; if you are using fresh herbs, chop fine. Add to the vegetables.

5. Add tomato juice, red wine vinegar, lemon juice, olive oil, hot sauce, salt, and black pepper. Stir and taste. Add more hot sauce, salt, and pepper as needed.

6. Chill for at least an hour before you garnish and serve. It's best after twenty-four hours; it's still crunchy, but the flavors are nicely married. It should keep in the refrigerator for up to five days.

ITALIAN VEGETABLE SOUP

12 -14 servings

1 tablespoon olive oil
1 yellow onion
4 – 5 ribs of celery
2 large carrots
2 bell peppers, yellow, red, or orange
1 zucchini
1 yellow squash
1/2 teaspoon fennel seed
1/2 teaspoon dried thyme
1 teaspoon dried Greek or Italian oregano
1/2 teaspoon dried basil
1/4 teaspoon dried red pepper flakes
1/8 teaspoon cinnamon
1/2 teaspoon salt
1/4 teaspoon white or black pepper
1 bay leaf
3 garlic cloves
2 cups sliced mushrooms
14 ounces canned, diced tomatoes
4 – 5 cups water or low–sodium vegetable broth
14 ounces canned cannellini beans, drained and rinsed
6 ounces tomato paste

Garnish

grated or shaved Parmesan cheese
fresh basil

1. Place olive oil in a large stockpot or Dutch oven.
2. As needed, peel, trim, stem, and core onion, celery, carrots, peppers, zucchini, and yellow squash. Chop in small-medium dice (1/4 - 1/2 inch square).
3. Place chopped vegetables in the stock pot and set it over medium heat. Add all the spices, herbs, and bay leaf. Sauté, stirring occasionally, until the vegetables begin to soften.
4. Peel and grate or finely chop the garlic cloves. Add to the stockpot.
5. Clean and slice mushrooms. Add to the stockpot.
6. Add diced tomatoes and cannellini beans.
7. Pour the water or broth into the stockpot. It should come up a couple inches above the vegetables in the pot.
8. Stir and bring to a low simmer over medium-high heat.
9. Stir in the tomato paste. Reduce heat to medium-low and simmer for 30 minutes before serving.
10. Garnish with Parmesan and fresh basil.

Use a vegetable peeler to cut thin strips from a block of Parmigiano Reggiano

CLAM CHOWDER

8 servings

6 tablespoons melted butter or vegetable oil

6 tablespoons all-purpose flour

12 ounces clam juice

2 cups milk, 2% or whole

12 - 14 ounces chopped/minced clams

*3 ounces bacon, cut into small bits

1 cup chopped white or yellow onion

1 cup diced celery

1 cup peeled and diced russet potatoes

1/2 tablespoon olive oil

1/4 teaspoon dried thyme

1/4 teaspoon dry mustard

1/2 teaspoon ground sage

1 bay leaf

3/4 teaspoon salt

3/4 teaspoon black pepper

1/4 cup white wine or water

1/2 cup heavy cream

* If you have precooked Bacon Bits (page 47), use about 3/4 cup

1. Mix the flour and melted butter or oil with a wire whisk to make a roux in a small bowl. Set aside.

2. Combine the milk, clam juice, and clams in a large saucepan or stockpot. Bring to a boil over medium heat. Watch and stir occasionally while you prepare the rest of the ingredients. Once it has reached boiling, turn the heat down so the broth is at a low simmer.

3. Cook the bacon bits in a large sauté pan or skillet over medium-high heat, stirring often. Once they are cooked through and browned, drain off the excess fat.

4. Add the onion, celery, potatoes, olive oil, thyme, dry mustard, sage, bay leaf, salt, and pepper to the pan with the bacon.

5. Cook the vegetables, stirring often, over medium-low heat for 15 - 20 minutes or until the potatoes are tender. Add the wine or water as needed to deglaze the pan if things are browning too quickly, or in the last few minutes of cooking.

6. Returning to your broth, turn up the heat and bring it to a boil again. Add the roux, stirring briskly with a wire whisk until fully combined. Stir and cook until the broth has thickened, about 5 minutes.

7. Stir in the cooked bacon and vegetables.

8. Finish by stirring in the heavy cream and keep warm until ready to serve.

Chef Billy recommends soaking potatoes in salted water if you prep them ahead of time so they don't turn brown.

Heceta Beach, Oregon Coast

CREAM OF MUSHROOM SOUP

8 servings

- 1 quart of chicken or vegetable stock
- 1/4 cup white wine
- 1 bay leaf
- 1 teaspoon dried basil leaves
- 1/2 teaspoon ground sage
- 1/2 teaspoon dried thyme leaves
- 1/2 teaspoon white pepper
- 1 teaspoon salt
- 6 tablespoons melted butter or vegetable oil
- 6 tablespoons all-purpose flour
- 1 tablespoon olive or canola oil
- 1 large yellow onion, chopped
- 2 ribs of celery, chopped
- 2 tablespoons chopped garlic
- 5 cups sliced crimini or white button mushrooms
- 1/2 cup heavy cream

1. In a large saucepan or stockpot, bring the chicken or vegetable stock, wine, bay leaf, basil, sage, thyme, white pepper, and salt to a boil over medium-high heat.
2. In a small bowl, stir the melted butter or oil with the flour to make a roux. Make sure the mixture is smooth with no lumps.
3. Using a wire whisk, stir the roux into the stock and continue to stir until the mixture is smooth and thoroughly combined. Turn the heat down to low. Allow the stock to simmer and thicken, stirring occasionally, while you prepare the vegetables and mushrooms.
4. Chop the onion and celery and place them in a large sauté pan with the cooking oil over medium heat. Cook, stirring occasionally, until they become soft but not browned.
5. Chop the garlic and slice the mushrooms while the onion and celery cook.
6. Add the garlic and mushrooms to the sauté pan. Continue to cook, stirring often, for another 5 minutes or until all the veggies are cooked.
7. Add the vegetables and mushrooms to the thickened stock.
8. Stir in the heavy cream.
9. Keep the soup warm until ready to serve.

SAUCES, SEASONINGS, & MARINADES

Cocktail Sauce 84

Tartar Sauce 84

Stoneground Mustard Sauce 84

Horseradish Sauce 84

Hollandaise Sauce 85

Honey Bourbon BBQ Sauce 86

Garlic Cream Sauce 86

Swiss Cheese Mornay Sauce 87

Bordelaise Sauce 88

Au Jus 88

Hazelnut Pesto 89

Cajun Seasoning 89

Red Wine Beef Marinade 90

Treehouse Chicken Marinade 91

The job of a chef requires physical stamina to withstand long hours in a hot kitchen, agility to multitask at a rapid pace, leadership skills, an eagle eye to direct staff, and, most of all, passion for creating beautiful, delicious food.

Patience is a rare bonus; it's no wonder chefs are often known for their hot tempers and overblown egos. The stress can bring out the worst in an otherwise charming person, and an overburdened chef can make the most confident waitstaff cower and hide.

Chef Billy had his not-so-cool moments, for sure, but for the most part, he handled the position with ease and fun. While our four siblings worked as waitstaff, bartenders, and management, I never regretted following in his footsteps and working the back of the house. Thirty years later, I still recall the thrill of pumping out food on a busy weekend night and the camaraderie I felt working with my brother. He would cut the intensity with his infectious humor, and we rode the high, singing along with the country music radio station until the last ticket was gone. The money was never as good, but the glory was great.

My brother's skills are, perhaps, most highlighted in this chapter. The sauces, toppings, and marinades created by a restaurant's head chef set it apart and give it its identity. Often the simplest combinations of ingredients, like those in the Treehouse's Chicken Marinade for the popular Poulet Grille, can elicit countless compliments and keep guests coming back for more. I love demystifying the process and sharing with friends how to elevate a cut of meat or fish with a smooth sauce, flavor-infusing marinade, or crunch of a topping. It's my absolute joy to offer you the signature flavors of Chef Billy's kitchen in this chapter.

Chef Steve Ficker, his mom, Mary Lou, and Chef Billy and his mom, Betty. Steve was Billy's second chef for many years, and the two remain close friends. Betty and Mary Lou were friends long before their sons worked together. They shared the duties of music ministry at St Paul's Church and put all their kids through the same Catholic schools.

Many of the dishes from other chapters in the book will indicate the use of one or more of the following recipes.

For example, the Garlic Cream sauce is used in Poulet Bechamel and a few of the pasta recipes; the Stone Ground Mustard Sauce is the base for Crab Cakes, and the Cajun Seasoning coats the Blackened Salmon and Cajun Chicken Sandwich. I encourage you to find your inner chef and use the sauces for what you like to cook. Use the Honey Barbecue Sauce with pulled pork, the Cocktail Sauce with fish and chips, and the Hazelnut Pesto to add flavor to pasta, salads, or soups. I've included detailed instructions and tips from Chef Billy with the confidence you will be able to whisk together a perfect Hollandaise Sauce for your guests and gather all the glory you deserve.

COCKTAIL SAUCE

1 1/2 cups (8 - 10 servings)

12 ounces chili sauce (bottled)

1 tablespoon prepared horseradish

2 teaspoons lemon juice

1 teaspoon Worcestershire sauce

1. Mix together all of the ingredients. Add more horseradish for additional heat if you so desire.
2. Serve on top of fresh crab or shrimp for a simple crab or shrimp cocktail. Or serve with Grilled Prawns (page 155) or Pan Fried Oysters (page 110).
3. Refrigerate for up to seven days.

STONE GROUND MUSTARD SAUCE

3/4 cup (4 servings)

1/2 cup mayonnaise or sour cream

3 tablespoons stone ground mustard

1 tablespoon Dijon mustard

1/2 teaspoon lemon juice

1/4 teaspoon finely chopped garlic

1. Whisk together all of the ingredients until smooth.
2. Use under Crab Cakes (page 152) or as a dipping sauce.
3. It may be refrigerated for three to five days.

TARTAR SAUCE

1 1/4 cups (8 - 10 servings)

1/2 cup mayonnaise

1/2 cup sour cream

1/4 cup dill pickle relish

1 tablespoon capers, drained

1 teaspoon lemon juice

1/4 teaspoon chopped garlic (or 1/8 teaspoon granulated garlic)

1/2 teaspoon Worcestershire sauce

pinch of granulated sugar

pinch of salt

pinch of ground black pepper

1. Mix together all of the ingredients. Taste and add more salt and pepper as needed.
2. Serve with Pan Fried Oysters (page 110) or fish and chips.
3. It may be refrigerated for three to five days.

HORSERADISH SAUCE

2 1/3 cups (10 - 12 servings)

2 cups sour cream

1/3 cup prepared horseradish

1 teaspoon Worcestershire sauce

1. Mix together all of the ingredients. Taste and add more horseradish if you want more heat.
2. Serve alongside Whiskey Cured Prime Rib (page 184) or Prime Rib Dip (page 98).
3. It may be refrigerated for three to five days.

HOLLANDAISE SAUCE

1 1/2 cups (6 - 8 servings)

1 cup butter, melted

8 egg yolks

juice from one lemon, strained

dash of cayenne pepper

hot water (tap is fine)

1. Separate the egg yolks from the whites, place them in a heat-proof bowl (stainless steel works well), add the lemon juice and cayenne pepper, and whisk together. Refrigerate the whites for another use.

2. Fill a saucepan or the bottom of a double boiler about a third of the way up with water. Place over medium heat and bring it to a low simmer. Turn the heat down to low.

3. Melt the butter in the microwave or over the stove and set aside.

4. Place the bowl with the egg yolks, lemon, and cayenne directly over (but not in) the simmering water and whisk vigorously until they are warm and begin to thicken a bit.

5. Add two tablespoons of hot water as you continue to whisk.

6. Whisk in the melted butter, pouring slowly but stirring quickly.

7. Once the sauce comes together to the desired consistency, remove the bowl from the heat. Cover to keep it warm until you are ready to serve it.

8. Place it back over the water to heat just before serving. If the sauce becomes too thick, you may thin it with a little more hot water.

9. Use on fish, Poulet Grille (page 173), or Eggs Benedict (page 40).

Egg Separating Tips

* Make sure your hands and the eggshells are clean before you begin the separating process. Most harmful bacteria resides on the outer shell.

* Carefully place the eggs in a bath of lukewarm tap water for five to ten minutes (the eggs will cool it quickly, so add more warm water as needed), then set them on a towel to dry. Bringing them to room temperature will help keep the yolk intact, and they won't freeze your hands.

* Break the egg and allow the whites to run through your fingers into a bowl while you hold on to the yolk, then put it in a separate bowl.

HONEY BOURBON BBQ SAUCE

approximately 2 cups

1 cup ketchup

1/4 cup apple cider vinegar

2 tablespoons bourbon

2 tablespoons honey

1/2 teaspoon finely chopped garlic

1/2 teaspoon salt

1/4 teaspoon curry powder

1/4 teaspoon paprika

1/4 teaspoon chili powder

1/8 teaspoon cayenne pepper

1/8 teaspoon cloves

2 - 4 tablespoons tomato paste

1. In a mixing bowl, stir all the ingredients until they are well combined. Adjust the amount of tomato paste until you achieve the consistency you desire.
2. Serve warm with beef, chicken, or pork.
3. Refrigerate for up to seven days.

Patrick's Barbecue Chicken, page 177

GARLIC CREAM SAUCE

approximately 2 cups

2 tablespoons butter

1/3 cup white or yellow onion, finely chopped

1 large clove of garlic, minced or grated

1 teaspoon salt

1/2 teaspoon white pepper

1/4 teaspoon dried basil

1/4 teaspoon dried sage

1/4 teaspoon dry mustard

2 tablespoons all-purpose flour

2 cups heavy cream (warmed in the microwave or on the stove to take the chill off)

1. Melt the butter in a saucepan over medium heat and add the onion and garlic. Sauté the onion and garlic for about five minutes until the onion softens and becomes translucent.
2. Stir in the salt, white pepper, basil, sage, and dry mustard. Continue to sauté for another few minutes or until the onion is fully cooked but not browned.
3. Sprinkle the flour over the cooked onions and seasonings and stir. Allow the flour to cook over medium heat for about 2 minutes. It will be clumpy.
4. Add the warmed heavy cream to the onion mixture 1/2 cup at a time. Stir until smooth after each addition.
5. Cook the sauce over medium heat until thickened. Serve immediately or refrigerate for up to three days.
6. Use in Poulet Bechamel (page 174), Vegetarian Lasagne (page 136), Pasta Melange (page 139), Prosciutto and Prawns (page 141), and Scallops Normandy (page 153).

SWISS CHEESE MORNAY SAUCE

approximately 3 cups

2 cups chicken stock, hot

3 tablespoons butter

3 tablespoons flour

1/4 teaspoon white pepper

1/2 teaspoon salt

1 egg yolk

2 tablespoons grated Parmesan cheese

1 cup grated Jarlsberg or Swiss cheese

1 tablespoon Dijon mustard

1/2 cup heavy cream

Ham Mornay sandwich, page 101

1. Heat the chicken stock in the microwave or over the stove until hot; set aside.

2. In a medium-large saucepan over medium heat, melt the butter and whisk in the flour to make a roux.

3. Stir in the white pepper and salt, and allow the roux to cook for a couple of minutes. Slowly, about 1/2 cup at a time, add the hot stock to the roux, whisking until smooth after each addition.

4. Bring the mixture to a low boil and cook, whisking often, until it has thickened.

5. Place the egg yolk in a small bowl and slowly whisk in about 1/2 cup of the thickened sauce to temper it.

6. Add the tempered yolk to the sauce and stir until well combined.

7. Stir in the Parmesan and Swiss cheese until it has fully melted.

8. Add the Dijon mustard and heavy cream and stir until the sauce is smooth.

9. Use the warm sauce on Eggs Mornay (page 40), Ham or Turkey Mornay sandwich (page 101), steamed broccoli or cauliflower.

10. Refrigerate for up to three days.

Decadent cheesy deliciousness

BORDELAISE SAUCE

approximately 2 cups

2 cups beef stock or broth

1/4 teaspoon chopped garlic

2 tablespoons red wine

1 tablespoon brandy

1/2 teaspoon salt

5 whole black peppercorns

1/4 teaspoon dried thyme

1 bay leaf

1/4 teaspoon fennel seed

1 tablespoon chopped parsley

1/8 teaspoon tarragon

1 tablespoon demi-glace, store bought

2 tablespoons cornstarch

1/4 cup water

1 cup chopped mushrooms

1. In a large saucepan, bring the beef stock, garlic, red wine, brandy, salt, peppercorns, thyme, bay leaf, fennel seed, parsley, and tarragon to a boil on medium-high.
2. Turn the heat down to low and allow the mixture to simmer for one hour.
3. Strain out the spices, then return the liquid to the saucepan and bring it to a boil.
4. Add the demi-glace and stir with a wire whisk until smooth.
5. Mix the cornstarch and water in a small bowl until no lumps remain.
6. Slowly whisk the cornstarch mixture into the sauce and cook over medium heat, stirring often, until the sauce has thickened.
7. Stir in chopped mushrooms.
8. Keep the sauce warm until serving time. It's delicious with Filet Mignon (page 187) or any cut of beef.
9. You may refrigerate it for up to five days.

AU JUS

approximately 2 cups

2 cups beef stock or broth

1/2 teaspoon chopped garlic

3 tablespoons red wine

1 bay leaf

1. Bring all the ingredients to a boil over medium-high heat in a medium saucepan.
2. Turn the heat down to low and allow the au jus to simmer for about 30 minutes. Keep warm or refrigerate for up to one week.

HAZELNUT PESTO

approximately 1 1/2 cups

2 cups fresh basil, packed

3/4 cup roasted hazelnuts (page 56)

2 cloves of garlic, peeled

1 tablespoon fresh lemon juice

1/2 teaspoon salt

1/2 teaspoon freshly ground black pepper

a small pinch of red pepper flakes

1/2 cup olive oil

1/2 cup shredded Parmesan cheese

1. Combine basil, hazelnuts, garlic, lemon juice, salt, black pepper, and red pepper in the bowl of a food processor (with a standard chopping blade) or blender.
2. Pulse or blend until ingredients are well combined.
3. Slowly add the olive oil and blend until the pesto is smooth.
4. Stir in the shredded Parmesan.
5. Refrigerate between uses; it should keep well for up to five days.
6. Use in Hazelnut Pesto Dip (page 115), pasta, dressings, sandwiches, and soups.

Cajun cooking was a huge trend in the 1990s.

Inspired by Louisiana Chef Paul Prudhomme, Chef Billy came up with his own cajun spice mix for an Elegant Evening. His blackened fresh salmon, halibut, and red snapper became instant favorites, and no one can beat his Cajun-style Pan Fried oysters.

He suggests you adjust the coating to your taste, whether cooking chicken, steak, or fish. For example, he enjoys the heat of a generous coating, so he cooks his protein first, then leaves it off for his partner, Liz, but cooks it in the same pan so she still enjoys the flavor without the intense heat.

CAJUN SEASONING

approximately 1 cup

1/4 cup paprika

1/4 cup cayenne pepper

2 1/2 tablespoons salt

2 1/2 tablespoons granulated sugar

2 1/2 teaspoons granulated garlic

1 1/4 teaspoons dried oregano

1 1/4 teaspoons dried thyme

1 1/4 teaspoons dried basil

1 1/4 teaspoons ground sage

1 1/4 teaspoons dried tarragon

1 1/4 teaspoons dried dill weed

1 1/4 teaspoons dry mustard

1. Stir all of the ingredients with a wire whisk in a mixing bowl. Make sure there are no lumps and the spices are thoroughly combined.
2. Store in an airtight container for up to one year.

RED WINE BEEF MARINADE

8 - 10 servings

3 pounds beef: chuck, sirloin, or flank

4 cloves garlic, peeled and sliced

1 tablespoon balsamic vinegar

3/4 cup red wine (something you would drink on a weeknight)

2 tablespoons olive oil

1 teaspoon kosher salt

freshly ground black pepper

Beef chunks marinating for Hearty Beef Stew, page 191

1. Trim and cut the beef according to how you will be using it. For stew and kebobs, a 1 1/2-inch cube works well. Flank steak can be left in one or two pieces.
2. Peel and slice garlic, 4 to 5 slices per clove.
3. Mix the balsamic vinegar, red wine, olive oil, salt, and pepper in a large glass or plastic bowl.
4. Add the beef and garlic to the marinade and make sure it is well combined.
5. Cover tightly or seal in a large plastic bag and refrigerate.
6. Allow the beef to marinate for at least 2 hours and up to 12 hours.

Cuts of beef vary for different dishes

* If you are making a stew or something that will braise for an hour or more, beef chuck is a good choice. It has more connective tissues, and the longer cooking time allows them to break down.

* Sirloin works well for a kebob, which will cook relatively quickly on the grill. A bottom sirloin cut, such as tri-tip, is a great, flavorful choice, but you could also use top sirloin for a more tender piece of meat.

* A flank steak that sits in this marinade for a while will be delicious grilled or broiled. Always slice flank steak against the grain for optimal tenderness.

TREEHOUSE CHICKEN MARINADE

8 - 10 servings

3 pounds boneless, skinless chicken breast

1 small or 1/2 large yellow onion

1/2 teaspoon salt

1/2 teaspoon white pepper

1 cup lemon juice, freshly squeezed or bottled pure lemon juice

2 tablespoons olive oil

1. Slice the chicken breasts diagonally in halves or thirds for 5 to 6-ounce filets, and pound them with a meat tenderizer mallet so they are uniform in thickness.

2. Place the chicken in a large bowl or plastic bag that can be tightly covered or sealed.

3. Peel and roughly chop the onion.

4. Add the onion, salt, pepper, lemon juice, and olive oil to the chicken.

5. Stir until the marinade is well combined and covers the chicken.

6. Refrigerate and marinate for at least 8 hours or up to 48 hours.

Poulet Grille, page 173

SANDWICHES & WRAPS

Poulet Grille Sandwich 96

Treehouse Club Sandwich 97

Prime Rib Dip with Caramelized Onions 98

Cajun Chicken Sandwich 100

Ham or Turkey Mornay Sandwich 101

Cheese Broils with Crab 102

Cajun California Wrap 103

Veggie Wrap 104

Salami Pizza Sandwich 105

Since he was a young kid, my brother, Billy, loved experimenting in the kitchen.

He often made elaborate after-school snacks for my sister, Suzanne, and me. The most memorable of those snacks was his signature "pizza sandwich." As all great inventions are, the pizza sandwich was born of necessity.

My brothers, Mike, Pat, and Bill, shared the converted garage of our ranch-style house in their adolescent and teen years. It was a large bedroom with a bathroom attached, separated by the laundry room from the galley kitchen that led to the rest of the house. Billy would often be woken up, not gently, in the middle of the night by our then-teenage brothers, Mike and Pat, who had come home hungry after a night out. To please them and avoid a late-night wrestling match, Billy put together the closest thing to a pizza he could.

This task was not easy, considering our mom kept a strict budget for household groceries. He took plain white bread, tomato paste, Italian seasonings, bologna or salami, and cheese and grilled them to perfection. At least enough perfection to satisfy his brothers' cravings and create a food memory still burned into his younger sister's brain forty years later.

Only a natural-born chef can pull off such a feat.

Alas, the Pizza Sandwich never made it onto a restaurant menu, but you'll find the recipe at the end of this chapter. Also included are favorites from the Treehouse and Billy Mac's, like the Prime Rib Dip, Poulet Grille, and Cajun California Wrap.

The Cheese Broil with Crab also had a humble beginning. Dad came up with it for him and Mom on New Year's Eve when they were in a small apartment with no money; only some sourdough bread and cheese. Little did he know it would become a favorite in our family for years to come. We serve it at Christmastime adorned with fresh Dungeness crab, and it was a popular item on Billy Mac's menu.

POULET GRILLE SANDWICH

2 sandwiches

2 chicken breasts, 4 – 5 ounces each
Treehouse Chicken Marinade (page 91)
2 slices sourdough bread
1/3 cup cream cheese, soft or whipped

1. Marinate the chicken in Treehouse Chicken Marinade for at least 8 hours.
2. Preheat a gas or charcoal grill to 375° - 400° F.
3. Cook the chicken breasts on the preheated grill for about 5 minutes per side, depending on thickness.
4. Toast the sourdough bread on a flat-top griddle or in a toaster.
5. Spread the softened cream cheese on the bread and place the grilled chicken breast on top.
6. Serve with a knife and fork.

Simply delicious!

TREEHOUSE CLUB SANDWICH

2 sandwiches

6 slices sourdough bread

2 teaspoons butter

4 – 6 slices cooked bacon (try Oven-Baked Bacon on page 46)

8 slices smoked ham

8 slices roasted turkey

2 leaves of lettuce, romaine or green leaf

4 – 6 slices ripe tomato

mayonnaise

1. Toast each slice of bread on a flat-top griddle (buttered first) or in a toaster (buttered after).

2. Heat the ham, turkey, and cooked bacon on the flat-top griddle or in a large sauté pan.

3. Spread the three slices of bread with mayonnaise and layer with ham and turkey on the top and bottom and bacon, lettuce, and tomato in the middle.

4. Cut into thirds.

Classic triple-decker sandwich

PRIME RIB DIP

4 sandwiches

4 French or hoagie rolls

2 teaspoons butter

12 – 16 ounces sliced Whiskey Cured Prime Rib (page 184) or other roast beef such as tri-tip

1 cup caramelized onions (page 99)

4 slices Swiss cheese

Au Jus (page 88)

Horseradish Sauce (page 84)

1. Lightly butter, then toast the rolls, each half cut side down on a flat-top griddle or cut side up in a toaster oven or under the oven broiler.

2. Divide the roast beef slices into four stacks and place them on a flat-top griddle or in a large sauté pan on medium-high heat. Turn each stack over once the meat on the bottom begins to brown.

3. Top each stack with a slice of Swiss cheese and about 1/4 cup of hot caramelized onions (warm them up if you've made them in advance) and heat until the cheese melts.

4. Place each stack of roast beef, cheese, and onion on a toasted roll.

5. Cut in half and serve with horseradish sauce, either on the sandwiches or on the side, and hot Au Jus for dipping the sandwiches.

CARAMELIZED ONIONS

approximately 2 cups

2 – 3 large sweet onions (like Walla Walla or Vidalia), peeled, halved, and sliced (should yield 4 – 5 cups)

2 tablespoons butter

1/2 teaspoon kosher salt

1. Place a large, heavy sauté pan or skillet (cast iron or stainless steel work well) over medium heat.

2. Add the butter.

3. Melt the butter, then add the sliced onions and salt.

4. Cook the onions over medium heat for 40 - 60 minutes, stirring often and lowering the heat as needed, so they don't cook too quickly. (The amount of time depends on how you intend to use them. You can pull them on the earlier side for sandwiches or keep cooking until they are further reduced and concentrated in flavor to top things like flatbreads.)

5. Use as needed and keep refrigerated for up to five days.

Slow-cooking the onions allows the juices they release to caramelize, producing a rich, sweet, complex flavor.

Use them in recipes like the French Dip (page 98) or Focaccia (page 32). You will likely have some left over to elevate everyday dishes like scrambled eggs and pasta.

CAJUN CHICKEN SANDWICH

2 sandwiches

2 chicken breasts, 4 – 5 ounces each

Treehouse Chicken Marinade (page 91)

2 – 3 tablespoons Cajun Seasoning (page 89)

2 tablespoons canola or vegetable oil

2 French sandwich rolls

2 – 4 tablespoons Garlic Aioli

4 slices Swiss cheese

1 tomato

2 – 4 lettuce leaves

Garlic Aioli

1/2 cup mayonnaise

1 clove garlic, grated or finely chopped

1/2 teaspoon dried tarragon

2 teaspoons red wine vinegar

1/8 teaspoon salt

pinch of black pepper

1. Pound chicken breasts until they are flat.
2. Marinate in Treehouse Chicken Marinade for at least 8 hours.
3. Coat the chicken with Cajun Seasoning.
4. Heat the oil in a large sauté pan or cast iron skillet over medium-high heat.
5. Carefully add the chicken in a single layer and cook for 3 - 5 minutes. Turn and cook for an additional 5 minutes or until the chicken is fully cooked. Remove from heat, cover, and keep warm while you assemble the remaining ingredients.
6. Toast the rolls and make the Garlic Aioli while the chicken cooks.
7. Slice the cheese and tomato.
8. Spread Garlic Aioli on the toasted bread.
9. Layer the sandwiches with chicken on the bottom, followed by tomatoes, lettuce, and cheese.
10. Cut in half and serve.

HAM OR TURKEY MORNAY

2 sandwiches

2/3 cup Swiss Cheese Mornay Sauce (page 87)

approximately 1 1/2 cups broccoli florets, steamed

2 slices sourdough bread, toasted

4 – 6 ounces sliced deli ham or turkey

1. Make the Swiss Cheese Mornay Sauce. (This can be made ahead and heated up.)
2. Steam the broccoli and pat it dry.
3. Toast the bread and heat the ham or turkey on a flat-top griddle or in a sauté pan on medium-high heat until it begins to brown.
4. Place the ham or turkey on the toasted bread, then the broccoli, and top it with the sauce.
5. Serve hot.

A delicious knife and fork open-faced sandwich!

CHEESE BROILS WITH CRAB

10 full servings or 20 appetizer servings

1/2 cup onion, minced
1 teaspoon olive oil
4 cups sharp or medium cheddar cheese, grated
1 tablespoon mustard, Dijon or spicy brown
1/3 – 1/2 cup sour cream or mayonnaise
1 tablespoon Worcestershire sauce
1/2 teaspoon horseradish
10 slices of sourdough or French bread
12 ounces of cooked lump crab meat

1. Peel and mince the onion.
2. Sauté on medium heat in the cooking oil until soft and just beginning to caramelize. Allow onions to cool while assembling other ingredients.
3. Place the grated cheese in a mixing bowl.
4. Add mustard, sour cream or mayonnaise (My sister and I use sour cream, Billy uses mayo like Dad), Worcestershire, and horseradish.
5. Add cooled onions and mix gently but thoroughly. A wooden or silicone spoon works nicely.
6. Spread a generous layer of the cheese mixture over each slice of bread.
7. Preheat oven to broil setting for a few minutes.
8. Place the cheese-covered bread on a sheet pan and broil for 5 – 7 minutes, checking often or until the cheese is bubbling and brown around the edges.
9. Top each slice with crab, distributing it evenly among the ten slices.
10. Cut in half or thirds and serve immediately.

CAJUN CALIFORNIA WRAP

2 wraps

2 chicken breasts, 3 – 4 ounces each
Treehouse Chicken Marinade (page 91)
2 – 3 tablespoons Cajun Seasoning (page 89)
2 tablespoons canola or vegetable oil
2 white or wheat tortillas, 14-inch
2 – 4 tablespoons Garlic Aioli (page 100)
4 slices cheddar cheese
1/2 avocado
2 – 4 lettuce leaves
1 small tomato

1. Pound the chicken breasts flat.
2. Marinate in Treehouse Chicken Marinade for at least 8 hours.
3. Coat the chicken with Cajun Seasoning.
4. Heat the oil in a large sauté pan or cast iron skillet over medium-high heat.
5. Carefully add the chicken in a single layer and cook for 3 - 5 minutes. Turn and cook for an additional 5 minutes or until the chicken is fully cooked.
6. Make the Garlic Aioli while the chicken cooks.
7. Remove the chicken from the heat and place it on a cutting board. Cut into strips.
8. Slice the avocado and tomato.
9. Divide the chicken between two tortillas. Top with Garlic Aioli, cheese, avocado, lettuce, and tomato.
10. Roll up the wrap and cut it in half.

VEGGIE WRAP

2 wraps

1/2 small yellow or white onion

1/2 bell pepper

4 – 6 mushrooms

1 tablespoon olive oil

2 – 4 tablespoons Garlic Aioli (page 100)

2 white or wheat tortillas, 14-inch

2 slices Swiss cheese

2 slices cheddar cheese

1/4 cucumber

1 small tomato

2 – 4 lettuce leaves (romaine or butter lettuce work well)

1. Slice the onion, bell pepper, and mushrooms.
2. Sauté the onion and bell pepper in the olive oil over medium heat until soft.
3. Add the mushrooms and continue to sauté for another few minutes until they are cooked.
4. Make the Garlic Aioli while the veggies are cooking.
5. Slice the cheese, cucumber, and tomato.
6. Spread the Garlic Aioli on each tortilla, then layer with the sautéed veggies, Swiss and cheddar cheese, cucumber, tomato, and lettuce.
7. Roll up the wrap and cut it in half.

SALAMI PIZZA SANDWICH

2 sandwiches

4 slices sourdough or Italian bread
1 – 2 tablespoons olive oil or melted butter
2 tablespoons Pizza Sauce
8 slices mozarella or provolone cheese
8 slices dry salami

1. Preheat a flat-top griddle on medium heat.
2. Brush each slice of bread with olive oil or melted butter on both sides.
3. Place each slice on the griddle and toast only one side of the bread until golden.
4. Remove from heat, and spread a layer of pizza sauce, two slices of cheese, and two slices of salami on the toasted side of each piece of bread.
5. Put them back on the griddle on medium heat and cook until the bottom side of the bread is toasted and the cheese has melted.
6. Put the slices together to form two sandwiches.
7. Cut in half and serve hot.

Pizza Sauce

1 6-ounce can tomato paste
1/2 teaspoon minced or grated garlic
1/2 teaspoon dried basil
1/2 teaspoon dried oregano
1 tablespoon warm water
pinch of salt
pinch of black pepper

Combine all of the ingredients in a small mixing bowl. Add a little more warm water, if necessary, to thin it out.

APPETIZERS

Pan Fried Oysters 110

Sautéed Mushrooms 111

Oysters on the Half Shell 113

Smoked Salmon Pâté 115

Hazelnut Pesto Dip 115

Hot Shrimp or Sweet Chili Shrimp 116

Crabby Mushrooms 117

Ginger Chicken Kebabs 118

Since I was old enough to remember, Dad would showcase his cooking skills on the twenty-fourth of December as he delightedly played host to dozens of friends at our annual Christmas Eve party.

My parents didn't entertain much at home beyond family gatherings. When they did, it was an event eagerly anticipated and fondly remembered by their guests, mostly neighbors and friends from church. They brought their children and grandchildren to celebrate with us as the years passed. The highlight of the evening was when my dad read Clement C. Moore's "The Night Before Christmas" in his booming voice to all the kids gathered around him next to the twenty-foot decorated Douglas or Noble Fir in our family room. We all headed to midnight mass at the evening's end.

My sister, Suzanne, and I would spend all day helping our mom clean and set up the dining room. We always served Ruffles potato chips, onion dip, and Mom's famous green punch consisting of lime cool-aid, 7-up, and a half-gallon of lime sherbet. After set-up, we allowed plenty of time to get dressed in our fanciest dresses, often borrowing my mom's rhinestone jewelry to be extra festive. When we returned to the kitchen, Dad would be in complete command as guests began to arrive, shouting about hot food.

Dad remained in the kitchen the entire evening, entertaining the guests as they watched him pull bubbling cheese broils and bacon-wrapped oysters and scallops that he called Angels on Horseback out of the oven. My brother, Pat, would tend the full bar set up in the pantry, and Billy would be beside Dad in the kitchen. The restaurant was closed for Christmas Eve and Christmas Day, and it was a wonderful time to be together as a family, entertaining our dearest friends.

The tree was lined with stuffed animals for the girls and t-shirts for the boys on Christmas morning. No matter how old we were or how big our family got, Santa always came.

After Dad passed, the party moved to Pat's house for several years, and then Billy took over. He still loves hosting his own Christmas Eve Party. In 2021, it was extra special as my siblings and our families gathered with close friends in Eugene for one last party at his restaurant, Billy Mac's, which had permanently closed the previous day.

Chef Billy may have retired from his restaurant days, but he will be cooking up a storm of heavy appetizers at his annual Christmas Eve parties for years to come.

His menu includes many of the recipes in this chapter. Oysters on the Half Shell, Hazelnut Pesto Dip, and Smoked Salmon Pâté are a few dishes his guests have come to expect. I can't resist his Cajun Pan Fried Oysters with Cocktail Sauce.

We cannot always be together on Christmas Eve, though my siblings and I, along with our families, often spend Christmas Day together. Still, wherever I am on the night before Christmas, I make a point to put on the fanciest dress the location will allow and pull some of my mom's rhinestone jewelry out of the drawer. And I always have a bowl of Ruffles potato chips and onion dip ready to share.

PAN FRIED OYSTERS

1 pound

one pound small or extra small oysters, shucked

Classic

1 cup all-purpose flour

2 teaspoons kosher salt

1 teaspoon black pepper

Cajun Style

1 cup all-purpose flour

2 tablespoons Cajun Seasoning (page 89)

3 tablespoons olive or canola oil

Additions/Garnish

Cocktail Sauce (page 84)

Tartar Sauce (page 84)

lemon wedges

1. Mix the flour and seasonings for classic or cajun style in a shallow bowl or on a plate.
2. Heat the olive or canola oil in a non-stick sauté pan on medium heat.
3. Coat the oysters in the flour mixture, then carefully place them in the pan, one at a time. (Use tongs to avoid hot oil on your fingers.)
4. Turn the heat to medium-high and cook for about 3 minutes per side.
5. Serve hot with cocktail sauce, tartar sauce, and lemon wedges.

Chef Billy likes to use oysters from Washington's Willapa Bay

SAUTÉED MUSHROOMS

2 to 4 servings

8 ounces whole white button or small crimini mushrooms

1 tablespoon olive or canola oil

1/2 cup white wine (something you might drink on a weeknight)

1 tablespoon cold butter

pinch of salt

pinch of freshly ground black pepper

1/4 cup grated parmesan cheese

fresh parsley. chopped

1. Clean the mushrooms with a damp paper towel, do not rinse or soak them in water.
2. Slice the tough end of the stem off of each mushroom.
3. Preheat the cooking oil in a large sauté pan over medium-high heat.
4. Add the mushrooms and sauté in the oil until they begin to brown. If they are browning too quickly, turn the heat down to medium.
5. Once the mushrooms are cooked through, add the white wine and cook over high heat until it releases the alcohol and reduces; this should take about two minutes.
6. Remove the pan from the heat and stir in the cold butter, salt, and pepper with the mushrooms and wine.
7. Transfer to a serving dish and top with parmesan cheese and fresh parsley.

Shucking Oysters

CHECK FOR FRESHNESS

* The shell should be completely closed.
* It should smell fresh and salty like the sea, not fishy.
* It should still be filled with seawater making it a nice heavy weight.

GATHER APPROPRIATE EQUIPMENT

* A brush for scrubbing the oysters
* A thick hand towel or oyster glove
* An oyster knife
* A bowl of ice to keep the oysters fresh

1. Scrub and rinse the oyster shell under running water.
2. Fold the towel so there is a thick layer to cover your hand or put the oyster glove on your hand to hold the oyster.
3. Find the curved side of the oyster and hold it, leaving the flatter side up.
4. Turn the pointed end of the oyster (commonly referred to as the hinge) toward you.
5. Make sure you have a good grip, then work the oyster knife into the hinge or down a little on the side until you find a spot you can pry open. Insert the knife about 3/4-inch into the oyster and, being careful not to break the shell, twist it back and forth until you have enough leverage to pop it open. Discard the top shell.
6. Check the oyster carefully for grit or loose shell. You can rinse (typical if you are cooking it) or lift the debris out with the tip of the knife to retain the flavorful liquid surrounding it (typical if you are serving it raw.)
7. Run the knife underneath the oyster to release it but leave it in the shell and place it on the ice while you shuck the remaining oysters.

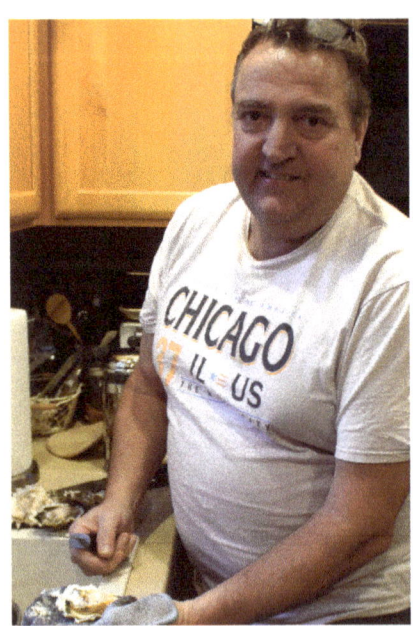

Chef Billy in my kitchen graciouly shucking oysters for our family Christmas dinner.

OYSTERS ON THE HALF SHELL

plan on 4 - 6 oysters per person

fresh oysters
shaved ice
lemon wedges
Cocktail Sauce (page 84)

1. Scrub and shuck the oysters. Use the tips on the opposite page as a guide.
2. Place the shaved ice on a platter or in a shallow bowl.
3. Place the oysters on the ice.
4. Serve immediately with lemon wedges and cocktail sauce.

Smoked Salmon Pâté is an impressive appetizer to serve your guests, requiring minimal effort.

Chef Billy shapes it into a fish with a slice of green olive for the eye. You can have fun using different shapes or molds or simply arrange it on a platter, as shown in the photo, with sliced baguette, then garnish with fresh herbs and lime wedges.

SMOKED SALMON PÂTÉ

approximately 6 servings

8 ounces smoked salmon

8 ounces cream cheese

juice of one lime (about 2 tablespoons)

Garnish (optional)

fresh herbs/dried dill/lime wedges

1. Break the smoked salmon into small chunks and place them in the bowl of a food processor. Pulse until the smoked salmon texture is smooth.

2. Cut the cream cheese into about six chunks and add it and the lime juice to the salmon. Blend until the mixture is smooth.

3. Transfer the paté to a serving platter or bowl and refrigerate for at least one hour before serving. If you are shaping or molding it, do that at this stage, then refrigerate.

Suggested Accompaniments

sliced baguette

crackers

Garlic Crostini (page 35)

sharp cheddar or dill havarti cheese

cucumber rounds

crudités

assorted olives

HAZELNUT PESTO DIP

approximately 6 servings

1/2 cup Hazelnut Pesto (page 89)

1 1/2 cups sour cream or Greek yogurt (or use a combination of both)

salt

1. Stir together the hazelnut pesto and sour cream/Greek yogurt. Add salt to your taste.

2. Serve with sourdough crostini or crackers and crudités.

This couldn't be easier to prepare, and it is always a crowd pleaser.

You can use any prepared pesto, but we are partial to the Hazelnut Pesto on page 89. The Greek yogurt is my addition to lighten it up a bit; it's great on its own or combined with sour cream.

Chef Billy hollows out a round loaf of sourdough bread and fills it with dip before serving

HOT SHRIMP OR SWEET CHILI SHRIMP

approximately 4 small servings

8 ounces of medium-sized shrimp (31 – 40 or 51 – 60 per pound)

1/2 cup cornstarch

canola oil or cooking spray

Sweet Chili Sauce or Hot Sauce

green onion, sliced

1. Prepare a deep fryer (350º F), air fryer (400ºF), or preheat a large sauté pan or skillet on medium-high heat.
2. Peel, devein, and remove the tail from the shrimp. (See tips on page 154.)
3. Place the cornstarch in a large bowl and toss the shrimp in it until fully coated. Shake off the excess.
4. If you use a deep fryer, drop the shrimp in the hot oil. If you're using an air fryer, coat the shrimp with cooking spray. In a sauté pan, heat about 1/4 cup of canola oil until it begins to smoke. Cook for 3 - 4 minutes, tossing and turning as needed, until golden brown.
5. Heat 1/3 cup of Sweet Chili Sauce or Hot Sauce in a large sauté pan or skillet.
6. Toss the fried shrimp in the sauce.
7. Garnish with green onions and serve hot.

Hot Sauce

1/4 cup hot sauce (Chef Billy suggests Frank's Redhot or Texas Pete's)

2 tablespoons fresh lime juice

1/2 teaspoon chopped garlic

Combine ingredients in a small bowl then transfer to a sauté pan to heat and toss the sauce with the fried shrimp.

Sweet Chili Sauce

3 tablespoons olive oil

3 tablespoons chopped garlic

1/2 cup red wine vinegar

1/2 cup sugar

3 tablespoons chili garlic sauce

15 ounces tomato sauce

2 teaspoons chili powder

1. In a large sauté pan, heat the olive oil over medium-low heat.
2. Cook the garlic in the oil until it is golden brown. Stir and watch it closely so it does not burn.
3. Add the sugar and vinegar and cook until the sugar has dissolved.
4. Add the chili garlic sauce, tomato sauce, and chili powder and simmer over low heat for 20 minutes. Set aside while you cook the shrimp.
5. You may make this ahead of time, and you will likely have leftover sauce. It will keep in the refrigerator for 5 - 7 days.

CRABBY MUSHROOMS

6 - 8 servings

20 – 30 white button or crimini mushrooms

1 pound Swiss cheese, grated

1/2 pound lump crab meat

1 egg, beaten

1/4 cup Dijon mustard

2 tablespoons bread crumbs

1 tablespoon dried dill

juice from one lemon (or 3 tablespoons)

1/2 teaspoon salt

pinch of black pepper

3 ounces white wine

1. Preheat oven to 375º F.
2. Clean the mushrooms with a damp paper towel and remove the stems.
3. Mix the grated Swiss cheese, crab meat, beaten egg, Dijon mustard, bread crumbs, dill, lemon juice, salt, and pepper together in a large bowl.
4. Stuff each mushroom with a generous amount of the crab mixture.
5. Use a baking pan that will allow the mushrooms to fit tightly and place the mushrooms in the pan.
6. Pour the white wine in to cover the bottom of the pan.
7. Bake for 15 - 20 minutes until the filling is browned.

GINGER CHICKEN KABABS

10 -12 servings

2 pounds boneless, skinless chicken thighs

MARINADE

2 cups pineapple juice

2/3 cup soy sauce

2 1/2 tablespoons Worcestershire sauce

1 1/2 tablespoons sesame oil

2 1/2 tablespoons fresh ginger, chopped

1 1/2 tablespoons garlic, chopped

1/2 teaspoon red chili flakes

1 tablespoon cornstarch

OPTIONAL

1 bell pepper (any color)

1 cup small pineapple chunks

1/2 yellow or white sweet onion

sesame seeds

chopped cilantro

1. Trim any excess fat off the chicken thighs and place them in a large container or ziplock bag.
2. Combine all marinade ingredients in a blender or food processor and blend until smooth.
3. Reserve 1 cup of the marinade and refrigerate it.
4. Pour the remaining marinade over the chicken thighs. Make sure the thighs are completely coated and seal the container. Refrigerate and marinate for 12 to 24 hours.
5. Soak 4-inch appetizer skewers in water for about 15 minutes.
6. Preheat a grill or oven to 400º F.
7. For oven baking, line a sheet pan with aluminum foil. (Optional: If you have a baking rack that fits the pan, place it on top of the foil and spray it with cooking spray.)
8. Cut the bell pepper, pineapple, and onion into 3/4-inch pieces and set aside.
9. Remove the chicken from the marinade onto a cutting board and shake off the excess. Use a sharp knife to cut the chicken into 3/4-inch cubes.
10. Thread the chunks of chicken, alternating with pieces of bell pepper/onion/pineapple, onto the skewers, beginning and ending with chicken. (Three to four chunks of chicken per skewer.)
11. Cook the kababs on the grill or in the oven for 15 to 20 minutes or until the chicken has cooked, turning once after 8 to 10 minutes.
12. Serve hot with a sprinkle of sesame seeds and chopped cilantro.

SIDE DISHES

Wild Rice Pilaf 124

Sautéed Vegetables 125

Twice-Baked Potatoes 126

Roasted Garlic Mashed Potatoes 127

Dad's Sausage Stuffing 128

When I think of side dishes, I often imagine a Thanksgiving table.

It's a meal that would be quite dull without the various savory and sweet bowls of vegetables, fruit, and starches to dish up alongside the turkey.

A holiday all about food and showing gratitude suited our dad perfectly. He loved to tell stories about the intense competition between him and his siblings when they got together for the big day. I can vividly picture my aunts, uncles, and Dad, who all had mad skills in the kitchen, arguing in loud but good-natured banter about whose turkey was the juiciest, whose stuffing was the tastiest, and whose pies were the flakiest. I've included Dad's Sausage Stuffing in this chapter because it's a family favorite always on our Thanksgiving table.

At the Treehouse, the Wild Rice Pilaf was served with seafood and chicken entrées, perfectly soaking up béchamel and hollandaise sauce. A decadent Twice Baked Potato accompanied the steaks and Whiskey Cured Prime Rib. Steamed or sautéed vegetables were on every plate.

Billy started making the Roasted Garlic Mashed Potatoes when he opened Billy Mac's, and they quickly became his most popular side. I love to make them at home to serve with Chicken Piccata or Dad's Burgundy Chicken. It's well worth the extra time to roast the garlic, and you'll find instructions on a simple way of doing that in the recipe.

Get creative and choose your side dishes with care to elevate your entrée and bring a fine dining experience home.

From left to right, Aunt Dolly (in the red shirt, sadly her face is hidden), Grandma Ina, Aunt Louise, Betty (Mom), Aunt Ruth

WILD RICE PILAF

10 - 12 servings

1 tablespoon butter

2 cups wild rice

1/2 teaspoon salt

1/4 teaspoon ground sage

1/4 teaspoon dried tarragon

1/8 teaspoon granulated garlic

1/8 teaspoon white pepper

3 cups water

2 cups chicken or vegetable stock

1. Melt the butter in a large saucepan over medium heat.//
2. Add the rice, salt, sage, tarragon, garlic, and white pepper. Sauté for 10 minutes, stirring often.
3. Add the water and stock to the rice and bring it to a low boil.
4. Cover, turn the heat to low, and allow the rice to cook for approximately 45 minutes.
5. Fluff with a fork and keep warm before serving.

SAUTÉED VEGETABLES

4 - 6 servings

1 medium zucchini

1 medium yellow squash

1 tablespoon olive oil

1 cup sliced mushrooms

a few leaves of kale, curly or Tuscan, sliced in thin ribbons

2 cloves of garlic, finely chopped or grated

a couple pinches of salt

freshly ground black pepper

1. Remove the ends of the zucchini and yellow squash. Slice each in half, lengthwise, then crosswise in thin half-circles.
2. Place the olive oil in a large sauté pan over medium heat.
3. Add the zucchini and yellow squash, then sauté for a few minutes while you slice the mushrooms.
4. Add the mushrooms and sauté, gently stirring or flipping the vegetables in the pan until they become soft and translucent.
5. Add the kale, garlic, salt, and pepper; sauté for a few more minutes.
6. Serve hot alongside your favorite entrée.

Change up this recipe with what you have on hand

* If you use vegetables that take longer to cook, like carrots, cauliflower, or broccoli, blanch them first or slice them very thinly.
* Toss in spinach and fresh herbs at the last minute.

TWICE-BAKED POTATOES

4 servings

- 2 medium russet potatoes
- 1/2 cup bacon bits (page 47)
- 2 tablespoons butter, soft or melted
- 1/2 cup shredded cheddar
- 1/4 cup grated Parmesan
- 1/4 cup sliced green onion
- 1/2 teaspoon salt
- 1/4 teaspoon black pepper
- 2 – 4 tablespoons warm milk or vegetable stock

1. Preheat oven to 400° F.
2. Scrub the potatoes and use a fork to pierce the skin about six times around each potato.
3. Place the potatoes directly on the rack or baking sheet in the oven. Bake for 50 - 60 minutes, until they are soft and easily pierced with a fork.
4. Prepare the bacon bits while the potatoes bake.
5. Allow the baked potatoes to cool slightly, then cut them in half, lengthwise, leaving the skins intact.
6. Scoop the centers into a mixing bowl and break them up with a fork before adding the remaining ingredients.
7. Add the bacon bits, butter, cheddar, Parmesan, green onion, salt, pepper, and 2 tablespoons milk or stock.
8. Stir with a large spoon until thoroughly combined.
9. Add more warm milk or vegetable stock if the mixture is too dry.
10. Fill the four potato skins with the mixture, mounding it on top.
11. Place them on a baking sheet and bake for 25 to 30 minutes, until they've browned on top.
12. Serve hot.

ROASTED GARLIC MASHED POTATOES

6 - 8 servings

1 head of garlic
1 tablespoon olive oil
3 pounds red or gold potatoes
pinch of salt
2 tablespoons butter
1/3 cup sour cream
1/2 cup hot milk
1 1/2 teaspoons salt
1/4 teaspoon black pepper
chopped parsley

1. Preheat oven to 400º F.
2. Remove excess peeling off the head of garlic but leave enough to keep it intact (It's ok if a few cloves get out of order). Use a sharp knife to cut it in half crosswise.
3. Place the garlic on a small sheet of foil and drizzle olive oil over each half. Wrap the foil loosely around the garlic and crimp the ends together so it's fully enclosed.
4. Bake for 40 - 45 minutes.
5. Scrub or peel the potatoes and cut them into quarters.
6. Place them in a large pot and fill it with water about two inches above the potatoes.
7. Bring to a boil over medium-high heat, throw in a good pinch of salt, cover, and continue to boil for 15-20 minutes or until tender. Adjust heat to prevent the water from boiling over.
8. When both the potatoes and the garlic are sufficiently cooked (A fork should easily pierce an individual potato when ready to remove from heat), drain the potatoes and place them in a large mixing bowl.
9. Squeeze or scoop the baked garlic from the peel and add it to the potatoes with butter, sour cream, milk, salt, and black pepper.
10. Vigorously mash the potatoes with a masher or electric mixer until the ingredients are well-combined.
11. Keep warm in a 200º F oven until ready to serve. Garnish with parsley.

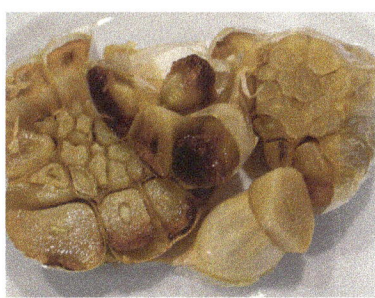

DAD'S SAUSAGE STUFFING

10 - 12 servings

*12 cups bread, cubed and dried (I like to use sourdough/ciabatta/Pugliese)

1 pound ground pork sausage

3 cups diced yellow or sweet onion

2 cups chopped celery

1 teaspoon sage, dried

1 teaspoon thyme, dried

1/2 teaspoon salt

freshly ground pepper

2 - 3 cups chicken or turkey stock

1 teaspoon fresh thyme, chopped

1 teaspoon fresh sage, chopped

1 teaspoon fresh rosemary, chopped

1/2 teaspoon nutmeg, grated or ground

2 eggs

1/4 cup butter

* 4 to 12 hours prior to making the stuffing, cut the bread into 1-inch cubes and place them on a sheet pan. Bake at 200º F for about 20 minutes, then leave them on the pan to cool and dry out.

1. Preheat oven to 350º F.
2. Brown the sausage over medium-high heat. (Use an oven-safe pan like a Dutch oven to do the browning and the baking, or use a separate sauté pan and an oven-safe 9x13-inch casserole dish.)
3. Chop the onion and celery while the sausage is cooking.
4. Transfer the cooked sausage to a paper towel-lined plate and set aside.
5. Add about 1 tablespoon of butter to the pan (don't clean it first, you want the brown bits), then add the onions, celery, dried sage, dried thyme, salt, and pepper.
6. Sauté until the onion and celery are cooked through and translucent.
7. Meanwhile, chop the fresh thyme, sage, and rosemary.
8. Place the prepared bread in a large mixing bowl and add the cooked sausage.
9. Add 1/2 cup of the stock to the onion and celery mixture to deglaze the pan, then add them to the bread and sausage.
10. Stir gently (be careful not to mush the bread too much) to combine. Stir in one cup of stock a little at a time. Stop if you think it's getting too wet because you will add more with the eggs at the end.
11. Add the herbs and nutmeg. Stir gently.
12. Taste it before you add the eggs. Add more salt, pepper, or herbs if necessary.
13. Add the last 1/2 cup of stock to the beaten eggs, then stir into the stuffing to combine. If it seems too dry, add a little more stock.
14. Generously coat the baking pan with butter.
15. Bake for 30 – 40 minutes. Cover with a lid or aluminum foil for the first 20 minutes, then remove it so it can get crispy on top.
16. Serve warm with turkey and gravy.

Dad always stuffed the turkey, but I prefer making it separately so, technically, it's "dressing." It cooks more evenly this way and has a nice crisp top.

PASTA

Grandma's Macaroni & Tomatoes 135

Vegetarian Lasagne   136

Pasta Melange 139

Fettuccini Alfredo 140

Prosciutto & Prawns 141

Pasta with Meat Sauce 142

Nancy's Tuna Noodle Casserole 143

One of the most satisfying things about working the sauté station in the Treehouse kitchen was making the fresh pasta dishes.

Little nests of fresh pasta cooked in boiling water while I quickly sautéed seafood for Pasta Melange or mushrooms for Fettuccini Alfredo and added the appropriate sauce. Then I'd toss in the pasta, top it with some chopped parsley and parmesan cheese, and have a beautiful entrée on the plate in about five minutes. It might take a little more time at home, but even if you use dried pasta and make the sauce from scratch, pasta is still one of the quickest, most versatile, and most pleasing dishes you can make.

Billy's Vegetarian Lasagna has been a staple at countless catering events. All of my nieces and nephews, whether they are vegetarians or not, are big fans who insisted I add it to this chapter. I also included my meat sauce recipe, which evolved from my mom's and is similar to Billy's. It's great in baked, cheesy pasta or on top of spaghetti or linguini. The last recipe in the chapter, Nancy's Tuna Noodle Casserole, is the most special to me.

In 1983, Nancy Petersen began waiting tables at the Treehouse, forever changing our family for the better.

She was a student at the U of O when she met Billy, the young head chef. They enjoyed twenty years of marriage before cancer took her way too soon in 2006. We all miss her terribly, but her quick wit and love of family live on in their three children, John, Abby, and Nicole. She often made her tuna casserole for me when I babysat, and I thought the cheesy biscuit topping was one of the best things I ever ate.
Though Billy was the chef, she could hold her own in the kitchen. Before she passed, Nancy dreamed of writing a cookbook for Billy, and I know she's been with me through the process.

Family comfort food: Grandma's Macaroni and Tomatoes

Billy and Nancy
Three Creeks Lake,
late 1980s

Use the recipes in this chapter as a guide to get creative and come up with your favorite combinations of meat, seafood, veggies, sauces, and pasta shapes. Any of the recipes will work with gluten-free pasta as well.

Nancy's Tuna Noodle Casserole

Tips for Cooking Pasta

* A couple of large pinches of kosher or table salt will season the pasta properly in the boiling water.

* Follow the cooking time on the package if you use dried pasta. Fresh pasta will cook in 3 - 5 minutes.

* Reserve a bit of the pasta water just before you drain it. Add a little as needed when you toss sauce and pasta together.

* Do not rinse the pasta. If you aren't immediately tossing it with a sauce, a little olive oil will keep it from sticking together once it's drained.

* Finish pasta dishes with fresh herbs for taste, texture, and presentation.

GRANDMA'S MACARONI & TOMATOES

8 servings

- 2 cups dried macaroni
- salt
- 12 ounces bacon
- 1 pound ground beef
- 1/2 teaspoon salt
- 1/4 teaspoon black pepper
- 1/2 teaspoon cinnamon
- 1/4 teaspoon allspice
- 1/4 teaspoon cloves
- 1 teaspoon dried oregano
- 1 large onion
- 1/2 green bell pepper
- 2 15-ounce cans diced or whole tomatoes
- 1 1/2 – 2 cups water (pasta water works best)
- 1 tablespoon granulated sugar
- 2 tablespoons tomato paste
- 2 tablespoons butter

1. Fill a stockpot 1/2 to 3/4 full of water and set it over high heat. Watch the water while you prepare the rest of the ingredients and add the macaroni and a few good pinches of salt once it boils.
2. Cook for about 11 minutes or follow the instructions on the package for al dente pasta. Reserve two cups of the pasta water then drain and set aside.
3. Cut the bacon into 1-inch strips. Place it in a large Dutch oven or skillet and cook over medium heat until the fat has rendered and the bacon is browned. Skim the fat before adding the ground beef.
4. Add the ground beef, salt, pepper, cinnamon, allspice, cloves, and oregano; break up the beef and stir occasionally until it's fully cooked.
5. Meanwhile, chop the onion and bell pepper into small dice.
6. Once the meat is cooked, add the chopped onion and bell pepper. Move the meat to one side or remove it from the pan to cook the vegetables efficiently. If you need to, add a little cooking oil or butter at this point. You may still have plenty of fat in the pan from the meat.
7. Once the onion and bell pepper are soft, combine them with the bacon and ground beef.
8. Add the diced or whole tomatoes, 1 1/2 cups water, sugar, and tomato paste. Bring the sauce to a simmer and break up whole tomatoes into pieces, if necessary.
9. Add the cooked macaroni and allow it to simmer for about twenty minutes. Add a bit more water if it seems too dry.
10. Stir in the butter and add salt and pepper to your taste before serving.

VEGETARIAN LASAGNE

8 servings

4 cups Garlic Cream Sauce
(page 86, double batch)

1 cup milk, heated

1/2 cup jarred sundried tomatoes, drained and chopped

10 to 12-ounce package of dried lasagne

1 medium yellow onion

1 red bell pepper

1 tablespoon olive oil

1 small/medium zucchini

1 small/medium yellow squash

2 cups sliced mushrooms

4 cups baby spinach

1/3 cup fresh basil

4 cups shredded mozzarella or provolone

1 cup crumbled feta

1/2 cup shredded parmesan

A delicious meatless option for parties!

1. Preheat oven to 350º F.

2. Make the **Garlic Cream Sauce** according to the recipe then stir the milk and chopped sun-dried tomatoes into the thickened sauce. Set aside.

3. Boil the lasagne according to the instructions on the package. Drain and use a little olive oil to keep the noodles from sticking together, then set aside.

4. Peel the onion, core the bell pepper, and slice them into strips.

5. Sauté the onion and pepper with olive oil in a large sauté pan over medium heat until soft.

6. Slice the zucchini and yellow squash into thin rounds. Slice the mushrooms and chop the spinach and the basil.

7. Generously coat a 9 x 11-inch casserole pan with cooking spray.

8. Spread about 3/4 cup of sauce on the bottom of the pan.

9. Add cooked lasagne noodles in a single layer over the sauce.

10. Spread 1 cup of sauce, and sprinkle 3/4 cup shredded mozzarella or provolone, 1/4 cup feta, and 1/4 cup parmesan over the lasagne noodles.

11. Layer one cup of sliced mushrooms, two cups of spinach, and half of the basil evenly over the cheese.

12. Add another layer of lasagne noodles.

13. Spread 3/4 cup of sauce over the noodles

14. Add half of the sautéed onions and peppers in a layer.

15. Add half of the sliced zucchini and yellow squash in a layer.

16. Add 1 cup of mozzarella or provolone and 1/4 cup of feta in a layer.

17. Add another layer of lasagne noodles.

18. Spread 1 cup sauce, and sprinkle 1/2 cup shredded mozzarella or provolone , 1/4 cup feta, and 1/4 cup parmesan over the lasagne noodles.

19. Add the remaining sliced mushrooms and spinach in a layer,

20. Add another layer of lasagne noodles.

21. Add the remaining sautéed onions and peppers in a layer.

22. Add the remaining sliced zucchini and yellow squash in a layer.

23. Add the final layer of lasagne noodles.

24. Add the remaining sauce, ensuring all the lasagne noodles are covered.

25. Top with the remaining mozzarella, feta, and basil.

26. Spray a sheet of aluminum foil with cooking spray and place it, cooking spray side down, over the lasagne. Make sure it's pinched on all sides but not too tight on the top so the cheese doesn't stick to the foil.

27. Bake for 1 hour. Remove the foil and continue to bake for another 15 minutes so the cheese bubbles and browns a little.

28. Allow the lasagne to rest for about 30 minutes before cutting and serving.

PASTA MELANGE

4 servings

1 cup Garlic Cream Sauce (page 86)

8 ounces linguini or fettuccini

1 – 2 tablespoons olive oil

12 – 16 ounces large shrimp

12 – 16 ounces *bay or sea scallops

1 cup dry white wine (sauvignon blanc or pinot gris)

2 tablespoons fresh lemon juice

1 tablespoon chopped parsley

* Bay scallops are smaller and will take less time to cook than sea scallops and shrimp.

See page 168 for sautéing tips

1. Make the Garlic Cream Sauce. Cut the recipe in half to yield 1 cup.
2. Bring a large stockpot of water to a rolling boil and add a couple good pinches of salt. Boil the pasta according to the directions on the package, then drain.
3. Peel and devein the shrimp (see tips on page 154).
4. Remove the tough muscle on each scallop's side; this may not be necessary with smaller bay scallops.
5. Measure the wine and lemon juice and chop the parsley so you have all your ingredients on hand.
6. Once the sauce and the pasta have cooked, heat the olive oil in a large sauté pan over medium heat.
7. Place the shrimp and scallops in the pan in a single layer with a bit of space between each piece.
8. Turn the heat up to medium-high and cook the shrimp and scallops for about 2 minutes, then turn and cook for another 2 minutes.
9. Add the wine to the pan and cook until it has reduced to about half its volume.
10. Add the lemon juice and the garlic cream sauce and stir to coat the shrimp and scallops.
11. Serve over pasta and garnish with chopped parsley.

FETTUCCINI ALFREDO

4 - 6 servings

8 ounces fettuccini

1 tablespoon olive oil
4 cups sliced white mushrooms
1/4 cup butter
1 1/2 tablespoons finely chopped garlic
1 1/2 cups sour cream
1/4 cup grated Parmesan cheese
1/2 teaspoon salt
1/4 teaspoon white pepper

chopped parsley
grated parmesan cheese

1. Bring a large stockpot of water to a rolling boil and add a couple good pinches of salt. Boil the fettuccini according to the directions on the package, then drain.

2. In a large sauté pan over medium-high heat, sauté the mushrooms in the olive oil until browned. Keep warm.

3. In a separate pan, melt the butter over medium-low heat. Add the garlic and allow it to cook for a few minutes. It should stay light golden in color.

4. Add the sour cream, Parmesan cheese, salt, and white pepper. Cook and stir until the cheese has melted and the sauce is smooth.

5. Toss the fettuccini and sautéed mushrooms in the sauce.

6. Garnish with parsley and Parmesan, and serve immediately.

PROSCIUTTO & PRAWNS

2 servings

3/4 cup Garlic Cream Sauce (page 86)

4 ounces linguini or fettuccini

5 – 6 slices of prosciutto

10 – 12 extra large or jumbo shrimp or prawns, peeled and deveined, tail on

2 tablespoons butter

1/4 cup brandy

chopped parsley

1. Make the Garlic Cream Sauce.
2. Bring a large stockpot of water to a rolling boil and add a couple good pinches of salt. Boil the pasta according to the directions on the package, then drain.
3. Tear each slice of prosciutto in half, lengthwise, and wrap each half around the individual **shrimp**; leave the tail exposed.
4. Melt the butter over medium heat in a large sauté pan.
5. Cook the wrapped shrimp in the butter for 3 - 4 minutes per side. The shrimp should be pink and the prosciutto nicely browned.
6. Turn the heat up to high and pour the brandy in with the shrimp. Allow the brandy to boil and reduce to about half it's volume, then turn the heat to medium.
7. Leave the brandy in the pan, remove the shrimp, and cover it with foil to keep it warm.
8. Stir the garlic cream sauce into the brandy in the sauté pan.
9. Divide the pasta between two plates. Top it with the sauce and 5 - 6 shrimp.
10. Garnish with chopped parsley and serve.

How to Peel and Devein, page 154

PASTA WITH MEAT SAUCE

8 - 10 servings

2 cups chopped yellow or white onion

1 cup chopped celery

1 - 2 tablespoons olive oil

2 teaspoons salt

2 teaspoons dried basil

2 teaspoons dried oregano

2 teaspoons dried parsley

1/4 teaspoon fennel seed

1/8 teaspoon red pepper flakes

1/8 teaspoon cinnamon

1 bay leaf

1 pound ground beef, turkey or pork

4 cloves garlic, peeled and finely chopped (about 1 tablespoon)

1 cup red wine

15-ounce can diced tomatoes

6-ounce can tomato paste

6 ounces water

fresh oregano, parsley, and/or basil

grated Parmesan cheese

1 pound pasta (spaghetti, linguini, or penne, etc.)

1. Chop onion and celery into small dice.
2. Place them in a large skillet, Dutch oven, or stock pot with olive oil over medium heat.
3. Add salt, basil, oregano, parsley, fennel seed, red pepper flakes, cinnamon, and bay leaf. Stir and saute until the onion and celery become tender and translucent, 8 – 10 minutes.
4. Add ground meat and chopped garlic; stir, and saute until the meat is browned. This should take another 10 – 12 minutes.
5. Add the wine and cook over medium-high heat for a few minutes to reduce and release the alcohol.
6. Stir in the diced tomatoes and tomato paste along with the water. If the sauce is still too thick, add a little more water. It will reduce as it simmers.
7. Cover and allow the sauce to simmer on low heat for about an hour; stir occasionally.
8. Bring a large stockpot of water to a rolling boil and add a couple good pinches of salt.
9. Boil pasta according to the directions on the package, then drain.
10. Chop fresh herbs for garnish.
11. Toss or top the cooked pasta with the meat sauce.
12. Garnish with fresh herbs and grated Parmesan cheese.

NANCY'S TUNA NOODLE CASSEROLE

6 - 8 servings

1 – 1 1/2 cups cooked macaroni or egg noodles
3 tablespoons butter
1 cup chopped onion
1/2 cup chopped celery
1/2 cup chopped red bell pepper
1 teaspoon salt
1/2 teaspoon black pepper
1/2 teaspoon granulated garlic
3 tablespoons all-purpose flour
1 cup vegetable broth
2 cups milk (heat it first for faster cooking)
1 cup sour cream
1/4 cup shredded Parmesan cheese
12 – 14 ounces canned tuna, drained
8-count package of refrigerated flaky biscuits
1 1/2 cups grated cheddar cheese

1. Cook and drain the pasta and set it aside.
2. Preheat oven to 350º F.
3. Melt 2 tablespoons of butter over medium heat in a large, oven-safe skillet or sauté pan and add the chopped onion, celery, and bell pepper.
4. Add the salt, pepper, and granulated garlic and cook until the vegetables are soft.
5. Add the remaining tablespoon of butter to the cooked vegetables. Once it has melted, sprinkle the flour over the vegetables and gently stir. Cook for a few minutes to combine the flour and butter.
6. Slowly stir in the vegetable broth, then the milk, stirring constantly to avoid lumps.
7. Cook until the sauce thickens, stirring often, for about ten minutes.
8. Stir in the sour cream and Parmesan cheese.
9. Add the tuna and pasta and continue to cook over medium-low heat while you prepare the biscuits.
10. If you need to transfer it into an oven-safe baking dish, do so at this point.
11. Roll each raw biscuit into a flat rectangle. Top with a layer of cheddar and roll into a log. Slice it into four round pieces.
12. Flatten each biscuit pinwheel slightly and gently place them atop the tuna noodle mixture until you've covered it entirely.
13. Bake for 45 - 50 minutes. The biscuits should be golden in color.
14. Let it rest for about ten minutes before serving.

SEAFOOD & LAKE FISH

Brown Sugar Glazed Salmon 148

Stuffed Halibut 150

Dungeness Crab Cakes 152

Scallops Normandy 153

Grilled Prawns or Shrimp 155

Corn Crusted Halibut with Avocado Salsa 156

Oysters a la Treehouse 158

Seafood Pan Roast 160

Blackened Salmon 161

Trout Almondine 162

Stuffed Trout 163

Siuslaw River Bridge
Florence, Oregon

The Oregon Coast has always been special to our family.

In the early 1950s, Betty Martin worked as a medical secretary in Portland, and she and her best friend, Patricia, would often take the short trip to the coast to spend the weekend. On one of those trips, she met Bill McCallum, a handsome US Coast Guardsman. He was two years her junior but lied and said he was two years older; otherwise, Betty would never have agreed to date him. Once she accepted his marriage proposal, he finally told her the truth, and, fortunately, she forgave him, or I wouldn't be here to tell you about it. However, she never let it go; it's literally the only detail I know about their courtship aside from the fact it began in a bar in Astoria.

As the years passed, my parents spent every chance they got on the coast. It was a quick drive from Eugene, so we made many day trips to Florence and spent a lot of nights in Yachats and Newport. Mom always insisted on a room with an ocean view. It is always beautiful, but often too windy and cold to spend much time on the beach, and she liked to hear the ocean. Dad required a kitchenette to prepare the fresh seafood he loved to pick up at the local fish markets.

Due to the ocean's proximity and Dad's passion, Dungeness crab, Yaquina Bay oysters, and Chinook salmon were featured prominently on the Treehouse menu, along with fresh halibut, scallops, and prawns.

The preparations ranged from simple to decadent; prawns charbroiled with lemon butter, stuffed baked halibut, and scallops finished in a delicate cream sauce, to name a few. The recipes in this chapter should work well with similar types of fish or shellfish, depending on what is available to you in your region.

Chef Billy has created countless nightly specials and has more preparations for seafood than could reasonably fit in this book.

The Corn Crusted Halibut with Avocado Salsa is a must-try, though, and the Seafood Pan Roast is a truly unique and delicious combination of flavors. It was a Billy Mac's favorite for a good reason. The broth is out of this world.

In addition to his affinity for the ocean, Bill McCallum was an avid fly fisherman. He had a whole room devoted to tying flies, and I would be remiss if I didn't give a nod to the mountain waters Dad loved and where he taught my brothers to fish. Rainbow trout was what they caught most in the high Cascade Mountain lakes, but he got very excited when they landed the brown-spotted Brook trout. "Brookies," he would say, were the best to eat. At camp, he pan-fried them with a simple seasoned flour, but at the Treehouse, the humble lake fish was prepared as Trout Almondine, and you'll find the recipe at the end of this chapter.

Billy, fly fishing for trout at Little Three Creeks Lake.
Mid 1970s

BROWN SUGAR GLAZED SALMON

4 servings plus extra glaze

4 salmon filets, 4 to 6 ounces each, fresh or frozen and thawed

Glaze

1 cup butter, melted

1 cup brown sugar

1 teaspoon lemon juice

1/2 teaspoon liquid smoke

1. Preheat oven to 375º F.

2. Place the butter in a small saucepan over medium heat. Melt the butter and add the brown sugar; stir until well combined.

3. Stir in the lemon juice and liquid smoke.

4. Set aside and allow to cool and thicken slightly.

5. Line a rimmed sheet pan with aluminum foil, or use a 9 x 13-inch baking pan coated with cooking spray.

6. Place the salmon fillets on the pan and spoon 1 - 2 tablespoons of glaze on each one.

7. Bake for 15 - 20 minutes.

8. Remove from the oven and serve with Wild Rice Pilaf (page 124).

Extra glaze will keep, refrigerated, for up to two weeks.

STUFFED HALIBUT

6 servings

6 halibut filets, 4 to 6 ounces each, fresh or frozen and thawed

1/3 cup white wine

*Dill Shallot Compound Butter

1/3 cup butter, softened but not melted

zest from one lemon

2 teaspoons fresh lemon juice

1 tablespoon minced shallot

2 teaspoons chopped fresh dill

salt

black pepper

Spinach Stuffing

4 cups baby spinach

1 tablespoon chopped fresh basil

1 garlic clove

salt

black pepper

5 ounces feta

*Make the Dill Shallot Butter at least one hour ahead of time, so it has time to chill.

1. Stir the soft butter, lemon zest, lemon juice, shallot, dill, and a pinch each of salt and pepper until well combined.
2. Place the compound butter on a sheet of plastic wrap and roll it into a log as you wrap it up. Chill in the refrigerator until it solidifies.
3. Preheat oven to 375º F.
4. Coat a 9 x 13-inch baking pan with olive oil.
5. Chop the spinach for the stuffing and place it in a mixing bowl.
6. Chop the basil and mince or grate the garlic and add them to the spinach.
7. Add the salt, pepper, and feta. Mix the stuffing with a wooden spoon until well combined.
8. Using a sharp knife, make a slit in the side of each halibut filet to form a pocket for the stuffing.
9. Fill each pocket with the spinach stuffing.
10. Place the stuffed halibut in the baking pan and pour the white wine to cover the bottom of the pan.
11. Bake for 15 minutes.
12. Slice the log of compound butter into 6 pieces.
13. Place a slice of compound butter on each halibut filet and bake for an additional 5 to 10 minutes.
14. Serve with Wild Rice Pilaf (page 124) and Sautéed Vegetables (page 125).

151

DUNGENESS CRAB CAKES

4 servings

1 pound lump crab meat, fresh or frozen and thawed

2 cups grated Swiss cheese

1 egg, beaten

1/4 cup mayonnaise

1/3 cup Dijon mustard

1/2 teaspoon dried dill weed

1 tablespoon lemon juice

1/2 teaspoon salt

1/4 teaspoon black pepper

1/2 cup bread crumbs

vegetable or olive oil

all-purpose flour for dredging

Stone Ground Mustard Sauce (page 84)

1. Mix the crab meat, grated Swiss cheese, egg, mayonnaise, Dijon mustard, dill, lemon juice, salt, and pepper with a large spoon.

2. Add the bread crumbs and stir until the mixture is firm and easy to form.

3. Form the crab cakes into thick flat discs, two to three inches in diameter. Make them smaller for appetizer portions.

4. Preheat the oil in a large sauté pan over medium-high heat.

5. Dredge each crab cake in flour, shaking off excess, and carefully place them in the hot oil. Be sure not to crowd the pan; you may need to work in batches.

6. Turn the crab cakes after two to three minutes and cook until they are golden brown on both sides. If the oil gets too hot, turn the temperature down to medium.

7. Serve over Stone Ground Mustard Sauce.

SCALLOPS NORMANDY

4 servings

1 cup Garlic Cream Sauce (page 86)

28 – 32 ounces sea scallops

2 tablespoons olive oil

2 cups sliced mushrooms

1 cup sweet white wine (riesling or Sauternes)

2 tablespoons lemon juice

2 tablespoons chopped parsley

lemon wedges

1. Make the Garlic Cream Sauce. Cut the recipe in half to yield 1 cup.

2. Find the tough muscle on the side of each scallop and remove it. It should peel right off.

3. Slice the mushrooms, measure the wine and lemon juice, chop the parsley, and slice lemon wedges so you have all your ingredients on hand.

4. Heat the olive oil in a large sauté pan over medium-high heat and add the mushrooms. Sauté until the mushrooms release their liquid and begin to brown.

5. Add the scallops and cook for about 2 minutes on each side until they are cooked through. Depending on the size of your pan, it might be necessary to remove the mushrooms, work in batches, or use an additional sauté pan so the scallops have plenty of room to cook.

6. Add the wine to the pan and cook with the mushrooms and scallops until it has reduced to about half its volume.

7. Add the lemon juice and the garlic cream sauce; stir to coat the mushrooms and scallops.

8. Garnish with parsley and serve immediately with lemon wedges. Wild Rice Pilaf (page 124) is a great choice for a side.

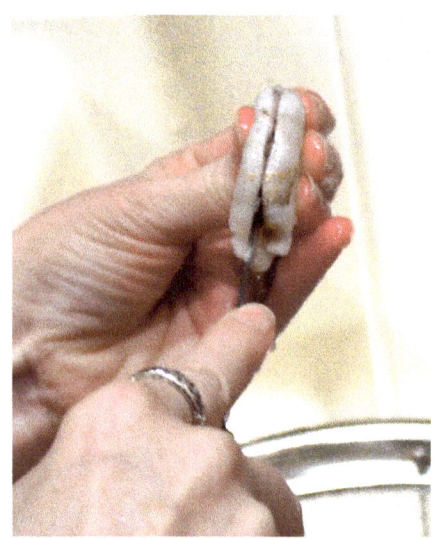
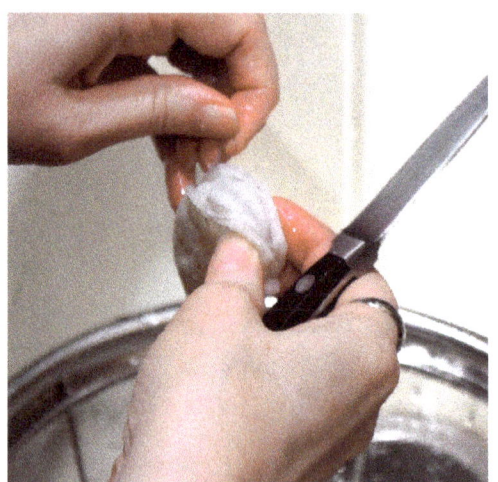

How to Peel and Devein Shrimp

* Using your fingers, dig into the bottom part of the shrimp, where the legs are, to release the shell. Peel the shrimp, leaving the tail on.

* Use a sharp paring knife to cut a shallow slit on the back of the shrimp, just deep enough to pull the grey/black vein out.

* Devein and rinse the shrimp under cold water, then place them on a clean towel or paper towel to dry.

GRILLED PRAWNS OR SHRIMP

4 - 6 servings

2 pounds extra large or jumbo shrimp or prawns, peeled and deveined, tail on

salt

black pepper

Lemon Butter

1/2 cup butter

juice of one lemon

Cocktail Sauce (page 84)

Note: If you use wooden skewers, soak them for about 30 minutes in water before use.

1. Preheat a gas or charcoal grill to 400° F.
2. Thread the shrimp onto the skewers and season them with a couple of pinches of salt and pepper.
3. Melt the butter on the stove or microwave, then whisk in the lemon juice.
4. Lightly brush the grill grate with cooking oil.
5. Place the skewered shrimp on the preheated grill and brush it with lemon butter.
6. Cook for about 2 minutes per side until cooked through and no longer translucent. Brush more lemon butter on the shrimp once you turn it, and once again just before serving.
7. Serve warm with Cocktail Sauce.

The title of this entrée on the Treehouse menu was "Prawns! Prawns! Prawns!"

I changed it because it seemed like a dramatic moniker for grilled shrimp. Prawns and shrimp are not technically the same animal but are used interchangeably in recipes, and I suspect what came out of the Treehouse kitchen were actually jumbo shrimp. Use whichever is available in your region.

CORN CRUSTED HALIBUT WITH AVOCADO SALSA

4 servings (with leftover salsa)

Avocado Salsa

4 ripe tomatoes, cored and diced

1/2 white or yellow onion, diced

1 red bell pepper, cored and diced

1 - 2 tablespoons sliced jarred jalapenos, chopped

1/2 cup cilantro, chopped

1/2 teaspoon salt

1/2 teaspoon sugar

1/4 teaspoon cayenne pepper

1/2 teaspoon ground cumin

1/4 teaspoon dried oregano

1/4 teaspoon basil leaves

2 tablespoons lime juice

1 ripe avocado, diced

1 tablespoon butter, soft

Corn Crusted Halibut

4 halibut filets, 5-6 ounces each

1 cup flour

1 teaspoon salt

1 teaspoon black pepper

1 cup buttermilk

2 cups cornmeal

1/4 cup vegetable or olive oil

1. Chop tomatoes, red onion, and bell pepper into small (1/4 - 1/3 inch) dice.

2. Place them in a large bowl and add the chopped jalapenos, cilantro, salt, cayenne pepper, cumin, oregano, basil, and lime juice. Stir and set aside.

3. Dice the avocado and place it in a bowl, separate from the salsa.

4. Mix flour with salt and pepper in a shallow bowl or on a plate.

5. Pour buttermilk into a shallow bowl.

6. Place corn meal in a shallow bowl or on a plate.

7. Dip all sides of each halibut filet in the flour mixture, then the buttermilk, then the cornmeal, and set them on a large plate.

8. Coat the bottom of a large saute pan with cooking oil and preheat for a few minutes over medium-high heat.

9. Place each coated halibut filet in the hot oil and cook for about 4 minutes per side until golden brown and cooked through.

10. While the fish is cooking, heat the salsa over medium heat. Just before serving, stir in the diced avocado and butter.

11. Serve the halibut with a generous topping of avocado salsa.

This was one of the few recipes from my brother I wasn't familiar with, but it became an instant favorite when I made it for the book. It tastes even better than it looks!

OYSTERS A LA TREEHOUSE

4 servings

24 –32 fresh oysters, cleaned and shucked
(See guide on page 112)

Oyster Butter

1 tablespoon butter

1/4 cup chopped green bell pepper

2 tablespoons chopped red bell pepper

1/4 cup chopped celery

2 garlic cloves, minced

1/2 cup baby spinach, packed

1 cup grated Swiss cheese

2 tablespoons grated Parmesan cheese

2 tablespoons sour cream

salt

black pepper

1. Preheat oven to 400º F.
2. Melt the butter in a large sauté pan over medium heat. Add the green and red bell pepper and celery and cook, stirring often, until the vegetables are soft but not browned, about three to five minutes.
3. Add the garlic and spinach and cook for an additional minute.
4. Place the cooked vegetables and butter into a food processor or high-speed blender and purée until the mixture is well combined.
5. Place the grated Swiss, Parmesan, and sour cream in a mixing bowl.
6. Add the pureed mixture and stir until well combined.
7. Clean and shuck the oysters.
8. Place about one tablespoon of the oyster butter on top of each oyster.
9. Bake for approximately 15 minutes or until the oyster butter is bubbling and browning nicely.
10. Serve immediately.

SEAFOOD PAN ROAST

4 servings

BROTH

8 ounces of clam juice, bottled

1/4 cup cocktail sauce (page 84)

1/2 – 1 cup white wine

2 tablespoons Worcestershire sauce

1/4 cup lemon juice

1 teaspoon smoked paprika

1 teaspoon dry mustard

1/2 teaspoon cayenne pepper

SEAFOOD

12 ounces total, any combination cod/rockfish/halibut/salmon

12 to 16 pieces total, any combination scallops/shrimp/clams/mussels/oysters

1 tablespoon butter

1/4 cup heavy whipping cream

lemon wedges

1. Combine the clam juice, cocktail sauce, 1/2 cup white wine, Worcestershire sauce, and lemon juice in a small saucepan. Whisk in the smoked paprika, dry mustard, and cayenne pepper.

2. Cook over medium heat, stirring often, and allow the sauce to simmer for a few minutes. Lower the heat and keep it warm while you prepare the fish.

3. Cut the fish into four or eight pieces to divide among four bowls.

4. Clean and prepare the shellfish, planning on three to four pieces divided among four bowls.

5. Place two large (10-inch) sauté pans over medium-high heat and divide the broth equally into each pan.

6. Add the shellfish that need to open up as they cook, like oysters, clams, or mussels, to the pans first. Divide them equally into the two pans, allow the broth to simmer, and bring them to the opening point. Add more white wine or water as needed if the broth reduces too much.

7. Once the shellfish is open, add the rest of the fish/shellfish and allow it to cook for one to two minutes per side.

8. Once the fish is cooked, add the butter and heavy whipping cream, dividing them equally among the two pans.

9. Cook on medium-high heat, shaking the pans gently to blend the butter and cream with the broth until the sauce is hot.

10. Serve immediately to prevent the fish from overcooking.

11. Divide the fish, shellfish, and sauce into four serving bowls. Garnish with lemon wedges and serve with baguette or other crusty bread to soak up the delicious broth.

Alternative versions shown on page 144

BLACKENED SALMON

2 servings

2 tablespoons canola oil
2 filets of salmon, 5 – 6 ounces each
1/2 to 2 tablespoons Cajun Seasoning (page 89)

Lemon Dill Sauce (optional)

1/2 cup sour cream or Greek yogurt
1 tablespoon fresh lemon juice
1/2 teaspoon dried dill
1/4 teaspoon granulated garlic
1/4 teaspoon salt

1. Make the Lemon Dill Sauce, if desired, by combining all of the ingredients in a small bowl. Set aside.
2. Preheat a large cast-iron skillet or sauté pan on medium heat.
3. Pat the salmon filets dry with a paper towel.
4. Coat each salmon filet with Cajun Seasoing. If you are sensitive to heat, opt for a light sprinkling instead.
5. Add the oil to the pan and allow it to heat up.
6. Place the salmon in the hot oil and cook for 3 to 4 minutes. Turn with a spatula and cook for another 3 to 4 minutes. Both sides should be nicely blackened, and the fish should flake easily.
7. Serve hot with the Lemon Dill Sauce or try it with Hollandaise Sauce (page 85).

TROUT ALMONDINE

4 servings

4 trout or steelhead filets, 5-6 ounces each, skin-on, deboned

1/2 cup all-purpose flour

1 teaspoon salt

1/4 teaspoon black pepper

2 tablespoons olive oil

1/2 yellow or white onion, chopped (about 3/4 cup)

1/2 green bell pepper, diced (about 1/2 cup)

2 cloves garlic, minced

1 shallot, minced

1/4 cup butter

1/2 cup sliced or chopped almonds

2 tablespoons lemon juice

lemon wedges

Dad with his catch of the day.
Bend, Oregon
mid-1940s

Fish for Mom

1. Mix the flour, salt, and pepper in a shallow bowl or on a plate.
2. Dredge the trout in the seasoned flour, coating each piece completely; shake off excess.
3. Heat one tablespoon olive oil in a large sauté pan or skillet on medium-high heat.
4. Sauté the onions and peppers in the oil until they are soft.
5. Push them to the side or remove them from the pan and add the remaining olive oil.
6. Brown the trout in the oil, 2-3 minutes per side, until golden and the fish flakes easily. Transfer the fish to a serving platter.
7. Melt the butter in the pan with the onions and peppers and add the almonds to toast until they've browned.
8. Stir in the lemon juice and add salt and pepper to your taste.
9. Pour the sauce over the trout and serve with lemon wedges.

Always watch for tiny bones when eating trout!

STUFFED TROUT

3 - 4 servings

2 whole rainbow or brook trout, butterflied and deboned

STUFFING

1 tablespoon olive oil

1/2 yellow or white onion, chopped (about 3/4 cup)

1/2 green bell pepper, diced (about 1/2 cup)

1/4 teaspoon salt

1/8 teaspoon black pepper

1/2 cup chopped mushrooms

3 cloves garlic, minced or grated

1 teaspoon lemon juice

2 tablespoons chopped roasted almonds

1 slice sourdough bread, cubed

2 tablespoons white wine

1. Preheat oven to 375º F.
2. Clean and debone the trout, if necessary. Ask the fishmonger to clean and debone it if you've bought it from a market.
3. Heat the olive oil in a large cast iron skillet or sauté pan.
4. Sauté the onions and peppers with salt and pepper in the oil until soft.
5. Add the mushrooms and garlic and sauté until they are cooked.
6. Stir in the lemon juice, almonds, and bread. Add more salt and pepper to your taste.
7. Fill the trout with the stuffing in the cast iron or a separate baking pan. Pour the white wine into the bottom of the pan.
8. Bake for 20 - 25 minutes. The fish should flake easily when done.

CHICKEN & PORK

Chicken Piccata 170

Chicken Marsala 172

Poulet Grille 173

Poulet Bechamel 174

Pork Saltimbocca 176

Patrick's Barbecue Chicken 177

Dad's Burgundy Chicken 178

Mom's Garlic Pork Roast 179

Faking smiles on a miserably hot day at a photo studio in the late 1970s.
Top: Pat, Bill, Mike, Cindy
Bottom: Molly, Betty, Bill, Suzanne

Our dad, Bill, and mom, Betty, were opposites in their approach to cooking.

The two recipes at the end of this chapter show off their different talents and purpose.

Mom always called herself a "utilitarian" cook. She did it because she had six kids to feed but did not particularly enjoy it. Her meals were simple, but they were always well-balanced and delicious. I have a great appreciation for the effort she put forth, especially on a tight budget. Having to come up with a meal for the family every night is tedious even for the most enthusiastic cook with two children. Mom's Garlic Pork Roast was always my favorite, and she taught me to stud it with sliced garlic cloves, which I still do when I cook it for my family.

Budget, duty, and nutritional value had no role in Dad's cooking, but passion certainly did. He was a true gourmet and took pleasure in more complicated and time-consuming dishes like his Burgundy Chicken, made with Burgundy wine from the four-liter jug that was a fixture on the pantry counter. I called it "purple chicken." It's nostalgic comfort food, and I love making it when I have the time.

Before I get to the popular entrées on the restaurant menus, I must acknowledge my brother Pat's recipe for Barbecue Chicken. It is not traditional, so if you are a barbecue purist, you might feel you have to skip it. If you want tender chicken with crispy skin that won't dry out on the grill while you worry about whether it's cooked through, be sure to try it. Discover the brilliance of Pat's method of baking the chicken in white wine before finishing it on the grill and covering it in a tasty sauce. It's the only way I cook bone-in chicken outdoors.

I hope you find the following recipes will help make feeding your loved ones more of a treat than a chore. Try Treehouse favorites like Poulet Grille, Poulet Bechamel, and Pork Saltimbocca. Or make Billy Mac's classics Chicken Marsala and Chicken Piccata.

This chapter includes tips for grilling, sautéing, and creating a perfect pan sauce. Try these techniques to confidently add a gourmet touch to your weeknight meals.

Sauté Tips

* The French term for gathering ingredients, measuring, chopping, etc., is "mise en place," and it's an important place to start. It's a good idea with any cooking or baking method, but it's essential before you begin the quick-paced sauté process so you can concentrate on the task at hand.

* Billy always uses the Treehouse Chicken Marinade on page 91 for his Chicken Marsala, Chicken Piccata, and Poulet Bechamel, and he suggests marinating the chicken for at least twelve hours. I also like to use it, but if I'm short on time, I still get a delicious finished product by seasoning the chicken with salt and pepper before cooking because the sauces are so flavorful. The exception to that shortcut is the Poulet Grille. It must be prepared with the Treehouse Chicken Marinade, or it's just another chicken skewer.

* Pull chicken or pork out of refrigeration at least fifteen minutes for cutlets and up to one hour for a large roast before browning.

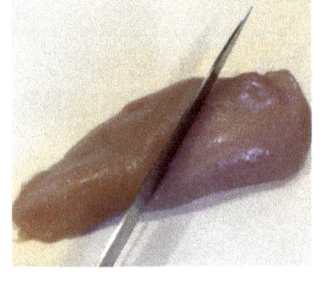

* Pat meat and fish dry with a paper towel to prevent steam, which will impede browning.

* Cut chicken breasts in half diagonally with a sharp knife, then pound with a mallet for uniformity in thickness to ensure even cooking time. Be patient with the pounding process; it might take several hits for a thick chicken breast to flatten. However, be careful not to overdo it, as it can shred or tear the chicken. I always cover them with a sheet of plastic wrap first.

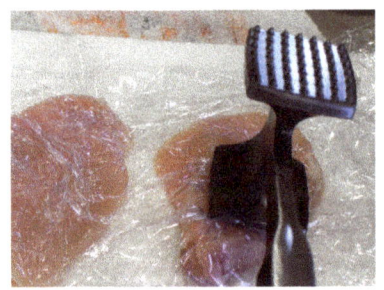

* Seasoned flour will add a nice texture when browning and help thicken a pan sauce. If you are avoiding wheat or gluten, you may omit it (the sauce will still taste great, it will just not be as thick) or use an alternative like rice flour or cornstarch.

* Don't crowd the sauté pan or skillet. The meat will not brown if it doesn't have adequate room, nor will fish or vegetables. Work in batches or use two separate pans if you are doubling a recipe or do not have the recommended-sized pan.

* To get a beautiful sear when cooking meat or fish, avoid turning it too early. It should easily release from the pan when it's ready to flip to the other side, so be patient if it's sticking.

* Every stovetop is different, so use the temperatures in the recipes as a guide. Turn your stove up or down if you feel it's cooking too slow or fast. You want a good sizzle for browning, but you don't want your meat or vegetables to burn. If they brown too quickly, toss a splash of wine, broth, stock, or water in the pan to deglaze and avoid burning, then proceed with cooking.

* If you are using mushrooms, keep in mind that they will produce excess liquid as they cook and shrink considerably.

* Garlic can burn quickly, especially if it's chopped or thinly sliced, so add it towards the end of the browning process, just before the liquids.

* Always add a liquid containing alcohol, such as wine, before other liquids, like broth or cream, when making a sauce. It needs to cook separately to effectively reduce and remove some of the alcohol.

* Finish sauces with butter or heavy cream, according to the recipe, adding them just in time to heat up and thicken the sauce. Fresh herbs should be the final ingredient, barely cooked or used as a garnish to retain color.

CHICKEN PICCATA

2 servings

2 chicken breasts, 5 – 6 ounces each

Treehouse Chicken Marinade (page 91)

1/3 cup all-purpose flour

1 teaspoon salt

1/4 teaspoon black pepper

2 – 3 tablespoons olive oil

1 teaspoon chopped garlic (1 – 2 cloves)

1 cup white wine

juice from one fresh lemon

2 tablespoons capers

4 tablespoons butter

pinch of salt

pinch of black pepper

3 tablespoons chopped parsley

1. Using a sharp knife, slice each chicken breast in half diagonally. You should have four approximately 3-ounce pieces.
2. Pound each piece of chicken with a meat-tenderizing mallet so they are all about the same thickness.
3. Marinate in Treehouse Chicken Marinade for at least 8 hours.
4. Mix the flour, salt, and pepper in a shallow bowl or on a plate.
5. Dredge the chicken in the seasoned flour, coating each piece completely.
6. Heat the olive oil in a 12-inch sauté pan or skillet on medium-high. Give it a minute or two to get hot, but not to the point of smoking.
7. Place each chicken breast in the hot oil and cook one side for four to five minutes or until nicely browned.
8. Turn the chicken and cook the other side for four to five minutes, adding the garlic about two minutes in.
9. With both sides browned, add the white wine and lemon juice.
10. Turn the heat up to high and allow the wine and lemon juice to reduce until the liquid is almost fully absorbed. Watch the pan closely and give it a shake when necessary.
11. Remove the chicken breasts from the pan, leaving the remaining liquid, and place them on two dinner plates.
12. Add the capers, butter, and parsley to the pan and stir until the butter is melted to finish the sauce.
13. Pour the sauce over the chicken breasts, dividing evenly between the two plates.
14. Serve with Wild Rice Pilaf (page 124), Garlic Mashed Potatoes (page 127), or pasta.

Chicken Piccata

Chicken Marsala

CHICKEN MARSALA

2 servings

- 2 chicken breasts, 5 – 6 ounces each
- Treehouse Chicken Marinade (page 91)
- 1/3 cup all-purpose flour
- 1 teaspoon salt
- 1/4 teaspoon black pepper
- 3 tablespoons olive oil
- 1 cup sliced yellow or white onion
- 8 ounces white or crimini mushrooms, sliced
- 2 – 3 tablespoons chopped garlic (6 – 8 cloves)
- 3/4 cup Marsala wine
- 1/2 cup heavy cream
- 2 tablespoons chopped fresh parsley

1. Using a sharp knife, slice each chicken breast in half diagonally. You should have four approximately 3-ounce pieces.
2. Pound each piece of chicken with a meat-tenderizing mallet so they are all about the same thickness.
3. Marinate in Treehouse Chicken Marinade for at least 8 hours.
4. Mix the flour, salt, and pepper in a shallow bowl or on a plate.
5. Dredge the chicken in the seasoned flour, coating each piece completely.
6. Heat the olive oil in a 12-inch sauté pan or skillet on medium-high. Give it a minute or two to get hot, but not to the point of smoking.
7. Place the chicken breasts in the pan, making sure there is space between them.
8. Add the sliced onions to the pan and allow them to cook, occasionally stirring with tongs, alongside the chicken.
9. The chicken should cook for 4 to 5 minutes per side or until golden brown.
10. Once the chicken is browned, add the mushrooms to the pan. Arrange the chicken breasts to be on top of the mushrooms and onions. Allow them to cook for a few minutes, stirring with tongs as needed.
11. Add the chopped garlic and allow it to cook with the mushrooms and onions for another minute.
12. Pour in the Marsala wine, bring it to a boil, and cook for about two minutes.
13. Stir in the heavy cream and parsley and cook until the sauce thickens.
14. Remove the chicken breasts from the pan, leaving the remaining sauce, and place them on two dinner plates. Pour the sauce over the chicken breasts, dividing evenly between the two plates.
15. Serve with Wild Rice Pilaf (page 124), Garlic Mashed Potatoes (page 127), or pasta.

Pictured on page 171

POULET GRILLE

4 servings

24 ounces chicken breast

Treehouse Chicken Marinade (page 91)

cooking oil

Hollandaise Sauce (page 85)

Wild Rice Pilaf (page 124)

Note: If you use wooden skewers, soak them for about 30 minutes in warm water before use.

1. Marinate the chicken in Treehouse Chicken Marinade for at least 8 hours.
2. Cut the chicken breast into 1 to 1 1/2-inch pieces.
3. Prepare hollandaise sauce; keep warm.
4. Preheat a gas or charcoal grill to 375º - 400º F.
5. Thread the chicken onto four skewers, so each has an equal amount.
6. Brush the grill with cooking oil.
7. Cook skewered chicken on the preheated grill for 10 - 12 minutes, turning halfway through until the chicken is nicely charred and thoroughly cooked.
8. Serve over wild rice with hollandaise sauce on the side.

Marinated grilled chicken and hollandaise sauce is a must-try combination!

POULET BECHAMEL

4 servings

24 ounces chicken breast

Treehouse Chicken Marinade (page 91)

1 – 2 tablespoons canola or olive oil

2 cups sliced crimini or white mushrooms

1/2 cup white wine

1 cup Garlic Cream Sauce (page 86)

1 cup grated Swiss, Jarlsberg, or Gruyere cheese

fresh chopped parsley or basil chiffonade

1. Cut the chicken breasts in half or in thirds, depending on size. Each piece should be 3 to 4 ounces.

2. Marinate in Treehouse Chicken Marinade for at least 8 hours.

3. Make the Garlic Cream Sauce. Set aside.

4. Preheat oven to 375º F.

5. Brown the chicken breasts in a large sauté pan, braiser, or Dutch oven over medium-high heat. Do not overcrowd the pan; you may need to brown half of the breasts at a time.

6. Remove them from the pan onto a separate plate when they are nicely browned and cooked most of the way through.

7. Add the sliced mushrooms to the pan and add more oil as needed. Sauté the mushrooms for a few minutes over medium-high heat until they begin to brown.

8. Add the white wine to the mushrooms and stir to deglaze the pan. Cook for a few minutes to reduce the wine.

9. If you plan to use the same pan in the oven, add the chicken breasts back to the pan with the mushrooms and white wine.

10. If you are using a separate baking pan, put the chicken breasts into it with the mushrooms and wine.

11. Spoon the Garlic Cream Sauce evenly over each piece of chicken.

12. Sprinkle the grated cheese evenly over the sauce-covered chicken.

13. Bake, uncovered, in the preheated oven for about 10 minutes. The sauce should be bubbling, and the chicken should be cooked through.

14. Remove the pan from the oven and allow it to rest for 5 to 10 minutes before serving.

15. Garnish with chopped parsley or basil chiffonade.

16. Serve with Wild Rice Pilaf (page 124) and Sautéed Vegetables (page 125).

Chiffonade: Leafy greens or herbs stacked, rolled, and sliced into thin, ribbon-like strips.

PORK SALTIMBOCCA

4 servings

- 24 ounces pork tenderloin
- 2 tablespoons olive oil
- 1/3 cup all-purpose flour
- 1 teaspoon salt
- 1/4 teaspoon black pepper
- 6 - 8 fresh sage leaves, chopped
- 1 teaspoon finely chopped or grated garlic
- 1/2 cup Marsala wine
- 4 tablespoons cold butter
- 2 - 3 slices prosciutto
- 4 slices fontina cheese

sage leaves or chopped parsley for garnish

1. Preheat oven to 350º F.
2. Divide the pork tenderloin into four 6-ounce pieces. Pound each with a mallet so they are flattened and about the same thickness (approximately 3/4 inch).
3. Heat the olive oil in an 18-inch sauté pan or cast-iron skillet over medium heat.
4. Mix the flour, salt, and pepper in a shallow bowl or on a plate.
5. Dredge the pork in the seasoned flour, coating each piece completely.
6. Place the pork in the hot oil, leaving space between each piece. Cook each side until nicely browned, 4 - 5 minutes.
7. Remove the browned pork and transfer it to an oven-safe pan.
8. Add the sage leaves and garlic to the sauté pan. Cook over medium heat for about a minute to brown the garlic, stirring often.
9. Add the Marsala wine to the sage and garlic. Allow it to cook and reduce to about one-third of its volume, stirring often to get all the browned bits deglazed from the pan.
10. Add the butter and stir into the wine sauce until just melted.
11. Pour the sauce over the pork.
12. Tear the prosciutto slices and divide evenly to top each piece of pork, followed by the fontina cheese.
13. Bake in the preheated oven for 15 - 20 minutes to melt the cheese and finish cooking the pork.
14. Serve with Garlic Mashed Potatoes (page 127) to soak up the delicious pan sauce.

Saltimbocca means "jump in the mouth" in Italian. A fitting description for the powerful flavors in this dish.

PATRICK'S BARBECUE CHICKEN

8 - 10 servings

5 – 6 pounds bone-in chicken (about 18 pieces; thighs and legs)

2 teaspoons salt

1 teaspoon smoked paprika

1 teaspoon freshly ground pepper

1 1/2 cups white wine

1 1/2 cups low-sodium chicken stock

2 bay leaves

4 – 6 large cloves of garlic

canola oil

1 cup barbecue sauce (try Honey Bourbon BBQ Sauce, page 86)

1. Preheat oven to 350º F.
2. Place chicken pieces in a large (at least 12 x 14-inch), deep-sided roasting pan or divide them between two 9 x 13-inch baking pans.
3. Trim excess skin and fat with a sharp knife or kitchen shears.
4. Mix salt, paprika, and black pepper in a small bowl. Sprinkle evenly over the chicken pieces, turning to get each side. Leave them skin side up to bake.
5. Peel the garlic cloves, then slice them lengthwise into two or three pieces.
6. Place the garlic slices evenly among the chicken pieces and add the bay leaves.
7. Add the wine and chicken stock. It should come up the sides of the chicken pieces about three-quarters of the way.
8. Cover the pan tightly with aluminum foil.
9. Bake for 1 hour.
10. Remove the chicken from the oven and allow it to rest while you preheat the grill.
11. Preheat a gas or charcoal grill to 375º - 400º F.
12. Line a separate baking sheet with paper towels and transfer the chicken onto the baking sheet to drain before grilling. This will reduce the steam on the grill.
13. Brush the chicken with canola oil, then place each piece, skin side down, on the grill. Reduce heat to 350º F and cook for about 5 minutes. Turn the chicken to skin side up, brush with sauce, grill another couple of minutes, then repeat so both sides have been sauced and grilled to caramelize the sauce. The total grill time should be no more than 10 - 15 minutes.
14. Place the hot chicken in a heat-proof serving pan and cover with aluminum foil. Allow the chicken to rest for 10 -15 minutes, then serve with more sauce and your favorite side dishes. Mom's Potato Salad (page 63) is a good choice.

DAD'S BURGUNDY CHICKEN

4 -6 servings

2 – 3 pounds chicken thighs, bone-in
3 tablespoons olive oil
1/2 cup all-purpose flour
1 teaspoon salt
1/4 teaspoon black pepper
10 ounces white button mushrooms, quartered
4 – 6 cloves of garlic, peeled and chopped
1 teaspoon chopped fresh rosemary
1 cup red wine
3/4 cup chicken stock
2 tablespoons butter, soft
2 tablespoons flour
chopped parsley (optional)

1. Preheat oven to 350º F.
2. Trim excess fat from the chicken thighs and pat them dry with a paper towel.
3. Heat olive oil over medium heat in a large, oven-proof skillet or Dutch oven.
4. Mix the flour, salt, and pepper in a shallow bowl or on a plate.
5. Dredge the chicken thighs in the seasoned flour, coating each piece completely.
6. Place the chicken in the hot oil, leaving space between each piece. Cook skin side down for about 10 minutes, or until golden brown. Flip and brown the other side for 6 - 8 minutes.
7. Transfer the chicken to a large plate.
8. Place the quartered mushrooms in the pan, adding more olive oil if needed. Cook over medium heat until they begin to brown, stirring often, for about 5 minutes.
9. Add the chopped garlic and cook for another minute.
10. Add the red wine and rosemary. Bring the wine to a boil and allow it to reduce to about half its volume.
11. Stir in the chicken stock.
12. Place the chicken thighs back in the pan with the mushrooms, wine, and chicken stock.
13. Cover and bake in the preheated oven for 45 minutes.
14. Remove the pan from the oven, remove the cover, and place it back on the stove over medium heat.
15. Mix the butter and flour together to make a paste, then stir it into the sauce. It should thicken up enough to nicely coat the chicken and mushrooms.
16. Place the chicken on a serving platter and spoon the sauce and mushrooms over it.
17. Garnish with chopped parsley.

MOM'S GARLIC PORK ROAST

6 - 8 servings

4-pound pork shoulder roast, bone-in or boneless
6 - 8 cloves of garlic, peeled
1 tablespoon kosher salt
1 teaspoon dried thyme
1 teaspoon dried rosemary
1/2 teaspoon black pepper
1 tablespoon olive oil

1. Season the roast (instructions follow) and allow it to sit at room temperature for 30 minutes, then preheat the oven to 450º F.
2. Firmly press down on each clove of garlic with the flat side of a large chef's knife to loosen the garlic peel and remove it from each clove. Slice each clove lengthwise into four to five thin but sturdy slices.
3. Mix the salt, pepper, thyme, and rosemary in a small bowl.
4. Use a small, sharp paring knife to cut a slit into the pork roast as long as a garlic slice. Insert a piece of garlic and press it into the roast. Repeat this process, leaving about two inches between each slit, all over the roast's top, bottom, and sides.
5. Rub the olive oil over the entire roast, apply the salt/herb mixture, and rub it all over the roast.
6. Place the roast on a rack in a roasting pan or baking pan.
7. Bake for 10 minutes at 450º F, then reduce the heat to 325º F and bake until a meat thermometer inserted in the thickest part of the roast reads at least 145º F. This should take about 2 hours, give or take 30 minutes, depending on your oven and the size of the roast.
8. Remove the roast from the oven and cover it with aluminum foil. Allow it to rest for about twenty minutes before slicing.
9. Slice and serve. Garnish with chopped parsley.

BEEF & LAMB

Whiskey Cured Prime Rib 184

Ribeye, Chargrilled or Blackened 186

Filet Mignon 187

New York Strip, Mushrooms & Blue Cheese 188

Brandied Pepper Steak 190

Hearty Beef Stew 191

Roasted Leg of Lamb, Rosemary Mint Au Jus 192

The best meal I ever ate was in front of a campfire in the summer of 1988.

I had joined my dad, mom, and longtime family friends, Fred and Mary Benoit, at our regular Three Creeks Lake campsite for what would be my dad's last camping trip, though I wasn't aware of it at the time. That evening, all I had on my mind was the food and the pleasure of the company.

Dr. Fred and Marybell Benoit were pioneers in the Oregon Wine Country scene and integral to its growth. They began growing grapes in the early 1970s and operated their Yamhill County winery, Chateau Benoit, from 1979 until their retirement in 1999. Their entrepreneurship wasn't the only thing they had in common with my parents; they also had six kids they put through the same Catholic schools in Eugene and shared a love for gourmet food and fine wine.

Dad and Mary took the reins preparing the food at camp that evening as Fred and Mom happily sipped Pinot Noir, and they all shared the easy conversation and laughter of old friends. Ever since I was a small child, I loved watching Mary cook in her beautiful Country French-style kitchen. I was happy to stand behind her as a student that night while she patiently caramelized Walla Walla Sweet onions to perfection in a cast iron pan on the Coleman stove. Meanwhile, my dad had generously seasoned a leg of lamb with salt, pepper, garlic, and fresh rosemary and was slowly roasting it over the fire coals. Creamy baby new potatoes rounded out the meal.

I remember thinking I never knew food could taste as good as it did that evening.

Tam McArthur Rim above Three Creeks Lake, Deschutes National Forest

In the absence of the rare campfire meal, I love to splurge on a night out at a great steakhouse, and I urge everyone to support their local restaurants. I also find it deeply gratifying to take a prime cut of meat you would pay four times as much for in a restaurant and know how to prepare it at home. This chapter is devoted to Chef Billy's recipes and tips for cooking ribeye steaks, filet mignon, and New York strips in the comfort of your home or the great outdoors. It also includes Whiskey Cured Prime Rib, perhaps the most beloved dish Billy has made consistently from his time at the Treehouse to our most recent family Christmas dinner.

I could never replicate Dad's fire-roasted lamb, but I've included my Roasted Leg of Lamb with Rosemary Mint Au Jus for you to try. My husband, Bob, didn't think he liked lamb, but preparing it with lots of garlic, fresh herbs, and an au jus sweetened with a hint of marionberry jam instead of a side of mint jelly changed his mind when I first made it several years ago, and even our picky seven-year-olds loved it.

Be sure to have plenty of Oregon Pinot Noir on hand with your steaks, roasts, and lamb, and always remember to toast your friends who are like family.

WHISKEY CURED PRIME RIB

4 - 6 servings

5 – 6 pound lip-on, boneless ribeye roast

1 1/2 tablespoons coarse black pepper

2 teaspoons dried rosemary leaves
(or 1 1/2 tablespoons fresh, chopped)

2 teaspoons dried thyme leaves
(or 1 1/2 tablespoons fresh, chopped)

1 cup coarse salt, kosher or rock

1/3 cup sour mash whiskey (like Jack Daniel's)

1. Place the roast in a roasting pan with sides at least one-inch high.
2. Rub the black pepper, rosemary, and thyme on the roast, covering the top entirely.
3. Cover the roast with the coarse salt, allowing it to mound up on top.
4. Slowly pour the whiskey evenly over the salt.
5. Allow the seasoned roast to sit at room temperature for at least one hour and up to two hours.
6. Preheat the oven to 350º F.
7. Place the roast in the preheated oven for 1 1/2 to 2 hours. Time will vary depending on the size of your roast and desired doneness; plan on at least 20 minutes per pound.
8. Use a meat thermometer inserted in the center of the roast to check the temperature. See the chart on the opposite page as a guide. Chef Billy suggests serving it medium-rare.
9. Pull the roast when it reaches the desired doneness and allow it to rest for at least 15 minutes before slicing. The temperature will rise five to ten degrees as it rests.
10. Carefully remove the salt crust, then carve the prime rib into thick slices.
11. Serve with Au Jus (page 88) and Horseradish Sauce (page 84).

Side note from Chef Billy:
"Most chefs don't like to cook steaks over medium because they lose most of the flavor of the beef."

Side note from me:
That's not how he used to say it behind the kitchen line.

TEMPERATURE CHART

Insert an instant-read or meat thermometer into the thickest part of the meat to get an accurate reading.

* Rare center: Remove from heat at 115° - 120° F for 125° serving temperature.

* Medium-rare center: Remove from heat at 120° - 125° F for 130° serving temperature.

* Medium center: Remove from heat at 130° - 135° F for 140° serving temperature.

* Medium-well center: Remove from heat at 140° F - 145° for 150° serving temperature.

* Well-done center: Remove from heat at 150° F - 155° for 160° serving temperature.

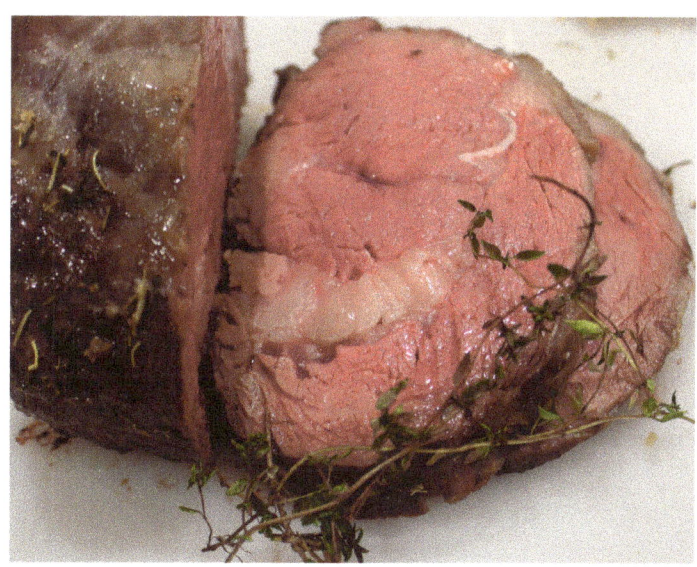

RIBEYE
GRILLED OR BLACKENED

2 - 4 servings

2 ribeye steaks, 10–12 ounces each, prime or choice grade

2 tablespoons olive oil

kosher salt

freshly ground black pepper

OPTIONAL

1 – 2 tablespoons Cajun Seasoning (page 89)

1. Remove the steaks from the refrigerator 30 minutes before cooking. Season them with salt and pepper.

5. Reduce the heat to medium and cook for 3 minutes per side until you get a nice, caramelized sear. (If your steak is thin, 3/4-inch, this should produce a medium-rare center.) Cook to the desired doneness. Use an instant-read thermometer to check the temperature; refer to the guide on page 185.

6. Allow the steaks to rest for 5 - 10 minutes before serving.

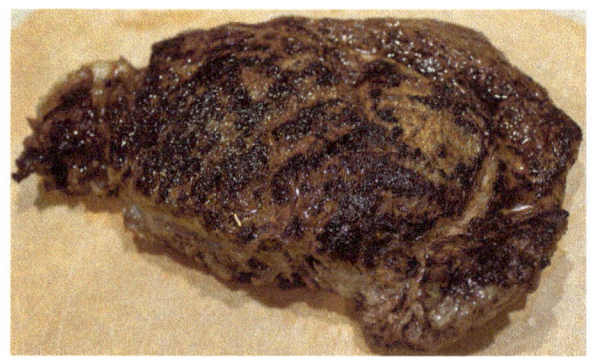

GRILLED/BARBECUED

7. Preheat a gas grill or barbecue to 400° F.

8. Rub the steaks with olive oil and place them on the grill.

9. Cook, covered for 3 minutes, then rotate (don't flip yet) and cook another 2 minutes for nice grill marks.

10. Flip and cook to the desired doneness using the temperature guide.

PAN SEARED/BLACKENED

2. Preheat a large cast iron, carbon steel, or stainless steel skillet or sauté pan on the stovetop on medium-high heat.

3. Coat the steaks with Cajun Seasoning for a spicy blackened steak.

4. Once the pan is hot, heat the olive oil, but don't let it smoke, then carefully put in your steaks, making sure not to crowd the pan.

FILET MIGNON

2 servings

2 filet mignon steaks, 6–8 ounces each, prime or choice grade

2 tablespoons olive oil

kosher salt

freshly ground black pepper

Bordelaise Sauce (page 88)

1. Follow the instructions for pan searing or grilling on the opposite page. The cooking time will depend on the thickness of the steak; use an instant-read thermometer and refer to the guide on page 185.
2. Top with Bordelaise Sauce (pictured on page 180).

A medium-rare steak will be soft to the touch when pressed in the center

"Remember, you can always fix a rare steak, but if you overcook it, that's dinner!"

– Chef Billy

NEW YORK STRIP WITH MUSHROOMS & BLUE CHEESE

2 - 4 servings

2 New York strip steaks, 14–16 ounces each, prime or choice grade

1 clove garlic, finely chopped or grated

2 sprigs fresh thyme

1 – 2 tablespoons olive oil

6 – 8 mushrooms, sliced thick

1/3 cup red wine

1 tablespoon butter

1/4 cup crumbled blue cheese

kosher salt

freshly ground black pepper

1. Remove the steaks from the refrigerator and place them on a large plate. Sprinkle generously on both sides with kosher salt (or another coarse salt).
2. Chop garlic and thyme.
3. Drizzle the olive oil over the steaks, then rub the oil, garlic, and thyme onto both sides. Cover with plastic wrap or foil and allow the steaks to rest for 30 minutes.
4. Meanwhile, clean the mushrooms with a damp paper towel, slice off the tough end of the stem, and slice lengthwise into pieces, 1/4-inch thick. Set aside.
5. Preheat a large cast iron, carbon steel, or stainless steel skillet or sauté pan on the stovetop on medium-high heat.
6. Once the pan is hot (a drop of water should sizzle and evaporate instantly), put in your steaks, making sure not to crowd the pan. Add more olive oil if necessary. Allow them to cook on each side for 2 – 3 minutes until you get a nice, caramelized sear.
7. Reduce the heat to medium and cook to the desired doneness. Use an instant-read thermometer to check the temperature; refer to the guide on page 185.
8. Remove the steaks from the pan and let them rest, covered with foil, while you prepare the mushrooms.
9. Place the pan back on the stovetop over medium heat and add the mushrooms.
10. Sauté the mushrooms until they begin to brown.
11. Once the mushrooms are mostly browned, add the red wine to deglaze the pan, stirring to lift up all the brown bits left from the steak. Cook over medium-high heat until the wine has reduced almost entirely.
12. Turn the heat off and add the butter.
13. Gently stir in the blue cheese crumbles, then top each portion of the steak with the mushrooms. Finish with a little more salt and freshly ground pepper.
14. Serve with Twice-Baked Potatoes (page 126) and Sautéed Vegetables (page 125).

Many prefer the rich flavor of a ribeye or a tender filet mignon, but the New York Strip is my favorite cut.

BRANDIED PEPPER STEAK

2 - 4 servings

2 ribeye steaks, 14–16 ounces each, prime or choice grade

1 teaspoon kosher salt

1 teaspoon minced or grated garlic

2 teaspoons coarsely ground black pepper

2 tablespoons olive oil

3/4 cup finely chopped bell pepper, any color

1/2 cup brandy

1/4 cup beef stock or broth

2 tablespoons heavy cream

chopped parsley (optional)

1. Remove the steaks from the refrigerator and place them on a large plate. Rub salt, garlic, and pepper generously on both sides.
2. Cover with plastic wrap or foil and allow the steaks to rest for 30 minutes.
3. Preheat a large cast iron, carbon steel, or stainless steel skillet or sauté pan on the stovetop on medium-high heat.
4. Once the pan is hot, heat the olive oil, but don't let it smoke, then add the steaks, making sure not to crowd the pan.
5. Reduce the heat to medium and allow them to cook on each side for 4 - 5 minutes to reach medium rare. Use an instant-read thermometer to check the temperature; refer to the guide on page 185.
6. Remove the steaks from the pan and let them rest, covered with foil, while you prepare the sauce.
7. Add the bell pepper and sauté, stirring frequently for 3 - 5 minutes, until soft.
8. Turn the heat up to medium-high and pour in the brandy (be careful, it will likely flame up). Allow it to boil off the alcohol and reduce it to about one-third of its volume.
9. Stir in the beef stock and a pinch of salt and bring to a simmer.
10. Stir in the cream to finish and pour the sauce over the steaks. Garnish with parsley.
11. Serve with Garlic Mashed Potatoes (page 127) and Sautéed Vegetables (page 125).

HEARTY BEEF STEW

10 - 12 servings

3 – 3 1/2 pounds beef, chuck or sirlion, cut into 1 1/4 inch cubes

Red Wine Beef Marinade (page 90)

1 – 2 tablespoons olive oil

1 yellow onion, peeled and chopped into large chunks

3 ribs of celery, chopped into large chunks

3 carrots, peeled and chopped into large chunks

6 red or white potatoes, chopped into large chunks

1/2 teaspoon kosher or sea salt

freshly ground black pepper

2 teaspoons dried thyme

1 teaspoon dried parsley

1 teaspoon dried oregano

1 bay leaf

2 – 3 cloves of garlic, peeled and minced

1 15-ounce can of diced tomatoes

1/2 cup red wine

1 1/2 – 2 cups low sodium beef stock or broth

3 cups sliced mushrooms

1. Marinate the beef in Red Wine Beef Marinade for at least 2 hours; 8 - 12 hours is best.
2. Remove the chunks of beef from the marinade and pat them dry with a paper towel to avoid steaming and promote browning.
3. Coat the bottom of a six to eight-quart stockpot or Dutch oven with oil and turn the heat to medium-high.
4. Brown the meat in two or three batches so it doesn't overcrowd the pan. Transfer the browned meat to another pan or bowl and set aside.
5. Add the chopped onion, celery, carrots, and potatoes to the pan you browned the meat in, along with a little more olive oil, if necessary. Allow the vegetables to sauté on medium heat, stirring often.
6. Add the salt, pepper, thyme, parsley, and oregano to the vegetables as they sauté. The vegetables don't need to cook long at this stage; they will cook thoroughly as they braise.
7. Add the meat back in and the bay leaf, garlic, diced tomatoes, and red wine. Turn the heat up to medium-high and bring the wine to a boil. Allow it to boil for a few minutes to reduce some of the alcohol.
8. Add enough stock or broth to come almost to the top of the meat and vegetables; it doesn't need to cover them completely.
9. Bring the liquid to a low boil on medium-high heat, then turn the heat down to low. Cover the pot and allow the stew to simmer for about an hour.
10. Stir in the sliced mushrooms and allow them to cook. This should only take about five minutes.
11. Taste the stew. Add more salt and pepper as needed.
12. Garnish with a sprig of fresh thyme and serve hot with Grandma's Rolls (page 25).

ROASTED LEG OF LAMB WITH ROSEMARY MINT AU JUS

8 - 10 servings

5-pound boneless leg of lamb

2 - 3 tablespoons kosher salt

1 whole head of garlic

1/4 cup olive oil

1 tablespoon fresh rosemary, chopped

1 tablespoon fresh thyme, chopped

zest from one lemon

freshly ground pepper

ROSEMARY MINT AU JUS

drippings from roasted lamb

1 cup red wine (malbec, pinot noir, or syrah would work well)

2 cups beef or lamb stock

2 sprigs of fresh mint

2 sprigs of fresh rosemary

3 - 4 sprigs of fresh thyme

1 - 2 tablespoons marionberry or blackberry jam

kosher or sea salt

freshly ground pepper

1. Pull the leg of lamb out of the refrigerator at least one hour before placing it in the oven. Liberally sprinkle kosher salt all over it.

2. Preheat oven to 400º F.

3. Slice the bottom off the head of garlic to release the cloves. Peel and slice each clove into 3 – 4 pieces lengthwise.

4. Drizzle about one tablespoon of the olive oil in the bottom of a large Dutch oven or roasting pan, then place the lamb in it, fatty side up, keeping the strings on.

5. With a thin, sharp knife, make about twenty slits, large enough for a slice of garlic, in the lamb leg, top, sides, and bottom.

6. Stick garlic slices into all the slits, then stuff the remaining garlic in the center. You want to make sure the garlic's not exposed or it will scorch, so really stuff it in there.

7. Combine the remaining olive oil, chopped rosemary, thyme, lemon zest, and freshly ground pepper in a small bowl.

8. Rub the mixture all over the lamb.

9. Place the lamb in the oven and roast at 400º F for 15 minutes to brown.

10. Turn the oven down to 250º F and roast for another 1 1/2 – 2 hours until a meat thermometer reaches 130º F (medium rare) or 140º F (medium). See the temperature chart on page 185 for guidance.

11. Remove the roast from the pan and place it on a large cutting board. Cover it with aluminum foil and allow it to rest for about 20 minutes.

Roast lamb was always on Dad and Mom's Easter dinner table

12. While the roast is resting, remove as much excess fat as possible from the bottom of the pan, leaving the good brown bits and juices. Transfer the pan to the stovetop.

13. Add red wine to deglaze the pan; stir and simmer on medium-high heat until slightly reduced, about 5 minutes. Then add the stock and fresh herbs. Bring to a simmer on medium heat and allow to cook, stirring occasionally, for 10 – 15 minutes.

14. Add salt and pepper to your taste and 1 tablespoon of the jam. Taste it before adding the second tablespoon; it may not be needed if you're using a fruitier wine.

15. Reduce heat to low and allow the au jus to simmer slightly while you carve the lamb.

16. Carve the lamb into thick slices with a sharp knife and transfer to a large serving platter.

17. Strain the au jus to remove the herbs.

18. Spoon a little au jus over the lamb and garnish with chopped fresh mint.

19. Transfer the remaining au jus to a small serving bowl to pass at the table.

DESSERTS

Whipped Cream 198

Raspberry Sauce 199

Treehouse Truffles 202

Dark Chocolate Mousse 204

White Chocolate Mousse 204

Chocolate Chunk Brownies 206

Creme Brûlée with Fresh Berries 208

Chocolate Dipped Strawberries 209

Bread Pudding with Bourbon Caramel Sauce 210

Chocolate Dipped Coconut Macaroons 211

One of my most delightfully ridiculous memories of working in the upstairs bakery at the Treehouse involves Hiron's Drugstore and a syringe.

I don't remember where the idea came from, probably one of my mom's Gourmet magazines. What I do recall is my then-boyfriend, Bob, racing from the restaurant across Franklin Boulevard to the drugstore. When he returned, he had procured the perfect tool for me to inject ripe strawberries that had been dipped in dark chocolate with Grand Marnier liqueur. The boozy strawberries became a summer staple on the dessert cart.

Bob and I met at the restaurant in the fall of 1987 when he began waiting tables. His charming, outgoing personality suited the job like my shy, sarcastic personality was best kept in the back of the house. Our three-year courtship began in that upstairs bakery, and we shared an additional thirty beautiful and adventurous years together until his sudden passing in January 2022. Of all the gifts the Treehouse brought me, he was the greatest.

Bread Pudding with Bourbon Caramel Sauce

My husband was my biggest champion. He wanted to make sure my talents were recognized, which was a big deal for me, as I had been fairly comfortable, if not content, in my supporting role as a little sister. When I began making Dark Chocolate Truffles, he built a refrigerated case to stand next to the front desk and insisted we make them available for easy take-out, complete with boxes and labels. He also had the idea to offer custom cakes for pick-up, and it became popular for customers to order them for birthdays and other special occasions. He did wonders for my self-esteem in those few years we worked together at the restaurant (and the decades that followed).

It's been so much fun revisiting recipes like White Chocolate Mousse, Bread Pudding, and Chocolate Chunk Brownies for this cookbook. My daughters, Ella and Hailey, have loved it, too; they inherited my sweet tooth and love of all things chocolate. They were incredulous that I'd been holding out on them as they watched me fold the large bowl of dark chocolate and whipped cream together for the silky Dark Chocolate Mousse, so I promised to make it again soon. I never retired the Chocolate Dipped Coconut Macaroons; they are in demand every Christmas as favorites on the cookie tray. The Creme Brûlée was never on the Treehouse dessert cart, but it would have been at home there. It was my mom's favorite thing to order when she dined out, so I made it for my recipe blog, AuntieChatter.com, one Mother's Day when I was missing her. Brûléeing sugar with a culinary torch never gets old.

Eating dessert is one of the true delights in life. It's comparable to feeling warm sand on your toes, sharing deep belly laughs with your best friend, and the feeling you get when the love of your life goes the extra mile just to see you shine.

Enjoy every delicious minute of it.

WHIPPED CREAM

approximately 3 cups

1 1/2 cups heavy cream

1/4 cup powdered sugar

1 teaspoon vanilla extract

1. Whip the cream in a stand mixer with the whisk attachment or with electric beaters until it's fluffy and can form soft peaks.
2. Add the powdered sugar and vanilla extract and beat until it is the consistency you desire.

It makes everything better

RASPBERRY SAUCE

approximately 2 cups

2 cups raspberries, fresh or frozen and thawed
1/2 cup granulated sugar
1 tablespoon lemon juice

Purée all the ingredients in a food processor or blender until smooth.

For: Dark or White Chocolate Mousse
Chocolate Truffle Cake
White Chocolate Cheesecake

Tempering Chocolate

Tempering chocolate can be intimidating and cause some confusion for the home baker, but don't let that stop you from tackling the chocolate-dipped recipes in this chapter. The two most important things to remember are not to let the chocolate get too hot or allow water or steam to make contact with the chocolate.

I use a simple method called seeding. It is helpful to have an instant-read thermometer, but not absolutely necessary. Considering that body temperature is around 98º F, you can use your sense of touch. Tempering will prevent unsightly blooming/discoloration and ensure a smooth, snappy texture.

Use a premium brand of dark chocolate with a cacao content of 60% to 70%. Good white chocolate will contain cocoa butter; avoid brands that substitute with alternative oils. Chop bars before melting or use baking discs.

* Melt about three-quarters of the total amount of chocolate called for in the recipe in the top of a double boiler over medium heat. You may also use a microwave-safe bowl and microwave the chocolate on high for short intervals, checking and stirring as you go, until the chocolate melts completely. It should be heated to approximately 120º F for dark chocolate, or 105º F for milk or white chocolate.

* Remove the chocolate from the heat and add the remaining chocolate. Stir with a rubber spatula until all of the chocolate has melted. Continue to stir until the chocolate is lukewarm, thick, and glossy. A temperature range of 95º F to 105º F is good for dipping. If you need to warm the chocolate up, do so over low heat in the double boiler or with short intervals in the microwave.

* Once dipped, refrigerate the confections until the chocolate solidifies and keep them chilled until you are ready to serve them. They should then be stable for at least several hours at room temperature.

* Use leftover dipping chocolate to make Dark Chocolate Ganache (page 216) or spread it out on some parchment paper and top it with nuts or dried fruit for chocolate bark.

TREEHOUSE TRUFFLES

10 - 12 truffles

GANACHE FILLING

8 ounces semisweet or bittersweet chocolate, chopped or discs

1/2 cup heavy cream

2 tablespoons butter, softened

pinch of sea salt

2 tablespoons liqueur (Amaretto, Hazelnut, Peppermint Schnapps, Grand Marnier, or Kahlua) or 1 tablespoon vanilla extract

CHOCOLATE COATING

16 ounces semisweet or bittersweet chocolate, chopped or discs

OPTIONAL TOPPINGS

1/3 cup toasted coconut (page 249)

2 tablespoons cocoa powder, for sifting

1/3 cup chopped nuts

2 ounces white or milk chocolate, melted

1 – 2 teaspoons flaky sea salt

1. Place 8 ounces of chocolate in a heat-safe bowl.
2. Heat the heavy cream in the microwave or on the stove. It should be hot enough to melt the chocolate but not boiling. Scrape off any "skin" that may have formed on top, then pour the cream over the top of the chocolate chips.
3. Stir with a wire whisk until all the chocolate has melted.
4. Add butter, salt, and liqueur or vanilla extract. Stir until smooth.
5. Chill the ganache in the refrigerator for about 2 hours, until the mixture is firm and can hold its shape. (You can speed up the process by placing the bowl of ganache over a larger bowl of ice, stirring with a rubber spatula until it thickens before you put it in the refrigerator.)
6. Fill a bowl with hot water and line a sheet pan that will fit in the refrigerator with parchment paper.
7. Dip a mini ice cream scoop or melon baller in the hot water, pat it dry, then scoop the ganache into balls approximately 1.5 inches in diameter onto the paper-lined sheet pan. Chill for at least another 30 minutes.
8. Prepare a double boiler. Fill the bottom with water so the top pan can rest over it, not submerged. Place it over medium heat.
9. Melt 12 ounces of chocolate in the top pan of the double boiler and stir until it is completely melted. Remove it from the heat.
10. Add the remaining 4 ounces of chocolate and stir until smooth and glossy. The chocolate should be warm but not hot, around 90º F. (See page 200 for tips on tempering chocolate.)
11. Line another sheet pan with parchment paper.
12. Prop a folded kitchen towel underneath one half of the chocolate pan so you have a deeper pool to dip from.

Prep the toppings before you begin dipping!

13. Use a dipping fork or wooden skewer to dip the chilled ganache center into the melted chocolate, then lightly tap it on the side of the pan to remove excess chocolate.

14. If you want to add a topping like chopped nuts or toasted coconut, roll the truffle in them before the chocolate hardens.

15. Place the truffle on the fresh paper-lined pan.

16. Use your finger to close up the hole left by the dipping fork or skewer with melted chocolate.

17. If you plan to sprinkle the truffles with sea salt or sift on cocoa powder, do so before they harden completely.

18. Chill truffles in the refrigerator until the coating is fully set and hardened.

19. If you are drizzling white or milk chocolate, do it after the coating has set, then place it back in the refrigerator to harden.

20. Keep the truffles chilled before serving.

DARK CHOCOLATE MOUSSE

6 -8 servings

4 eggs, separated

1 tablespoon granulated sugar

10 ounces semisweet chocolate, chopped or discs

3 tablespoons dark rum, triple sec, or coffee liqueur

16 ounces heavy cream

WHITE CHOCOLATE MOUSSE

6 -8 servings

4 eggs, separated

1 tablespoon granulated sugar

8 ounces white chocolate, chopped or discs

4 teaspoons butter

3 tablespoons triple sec or Irish cream liqueur

16 ounces heavy cream

See Tips for Separating Eggs on page 85

Use the following instructions for Dark Chocolate or White Chocolate Mousse.

1. Separate the eggs and place the whites and yolks into two separate mixing bowls.

2. Use an electric mixer to beat the whites until they form soft peaks. Add the sugar and continue beating until they become glossy and form stiff peaks. Set aside.

3. Clean the mixer beaters, then beat the yolks until they become thick and pale yellow.

4. Melt about two-thirds of the chocolate in a double boiler or a microwave. Remove it from the heat and stir in the remaining chocolate. Add the butter to the white chocolate. It should be warm, but not too hot, you don't want to cook the eggs.

5. Transfer the warm chocolate to a large mixing bowl and gently fold in the egg yolks using a rubber spatula. Once fully combined, gently fold in the egg whites.

6. Whip the heavy cream until it's thick and holds its shape.

7. Add the liqueur and whipped cream to the chocolate mixture and gently fold until thoroughly combined.

8. Chill in the refrigerator.

9. Serve on its own or top it with fresh fruit, Raspberry Sauce (page 199) shaved chocolate, and/or Whipped Cream (page 198). You can also use it as a cake filling.

Folding:

Use a light touch and a lifting, then spreading motion with a rubber spatula to combine delicate ingredients, like egg whites or whipped cream, with heavier mixtures. Regular stirring will deflate the lighter components.

CHOCOLATE CHUNK BROWNIES

16 brownies

1 cup butter, softened to room temp

1 cup brown sugar

3 eggs

1 teaspoon vanilla extract

1/2 cup unsweetened cocoa powder

3/4 cup + 2 tablespoons all-purpose flour

1/2 teaspoon sea salt

8 ounces semisweet chocolate, chopped or discs, divided

6 ounces white chocolate, chopped or discs, divided

1 cup roasted hazelnuts or pecans, chopped

Topping

2 ounces white chocolate, melted

1/2 cup roasted hazelnuts or pecans, chopped

1. Preheat oven to 350º F.
2. Coat a 9 x 13-inch rimmed pan with butter or non-stick spray, or line it with parchment paper.
3. Cream together the butter and brown sugar until light and fluffy in a large mixing bowl or the bowl of a stand mixer.
4. Add eggs, one at a time, and mix well after each addition.
5. Add vanilla extract.
6. Whisk the cocoa powder, flour, and salt in a separate bowl.
7. Mix the flour mixture into the butter mixture until combined.
8. Add 4 ounces of semi-sweet chocolate, 3 ounces of white chocolate, and 1 cup of chopped nuts. Mix until combined.
9. Spread the batter evenly into the prepared pan.
10. Arrange the remaining 4 ounces of semi-sweet chocolate and 3 ounces of white chocolate evenly over the batter.
11. Bake in the preheated oven for 14 - 16 minutes.
12. Melt the white chocolate for the topping.
13. Remove the brownies from the oven.
14. Drizzle the white chocolate over the brownies and sprinkle on the 1/2 cup of chopped nuts. Gently press the nuts in the melted chocolate.
15. Cut the brownies before they cool completely.
16. Serve warm with vanilla ice cream.

Roast and skin Hazelnuts, page 56

CRÈME BRÛLÉE WITH BERRIES

8 servings

4 cups heavy cream

1 vanilla bean, split and scraped

1 cup granulated sugar, divided

6 large egg yolks

1 teaspoon vanilla extract

2 cups fresh berries

1. Preheat oven to 325° F.
2. Place the heavy cream in a saucepan over medium-high heat.
3. Split the vanilla bean lengthwise with a small, sharp knife, scrape out the pulp with a teaspoon or table knife, and add the bean and the pulp to the heavy cream.
4. Bring the mixture to a boil, remove it from the heat, cover the pan, and allow the vanilla bean to steep in the hot cream for fifteen minutes.
5. Separate the eggs and place the yolks in a large mixing bowl. Refrigerate the egg whites for another use.
6. Add 1/2 cup of the sugar to the yolks and whisk briskly with a wire whisk until the mixture lightens in color and drizzles off the whisk in a thick ribbon.
7. Remove the vanilla bean from the cream and skim off any skin that has formed.
8. Whisk the hot cream into the yolks a little at a time to prevent the mixture from curdling, constantly stirring until thoroughly combined.
9. Add the vanilla extract.
10. Divide the custard evenly among eight 6-ounce oven-safe ramekins.
11. Place the ramekins in a large, high-sided baking pan and fill it with warm tap water to come halfway up the ramekins. This will allow the custard to bake gently and evenly.
12. Bake until the custard is set but trembling slightly in the middle, about 40- 45 minutes.
13. Remove the ramekins from the pan and allow the custard to sit at room temperature for thirty minutes. Refrigerate until chilled, at least 1 hour, or overnight.
14. Sprinkle 1 tablespoon of sugar evenly over the top of each custard. Using a chef's torch, melt the sugar until it is caramelized, or place the custards about 3 inches below the top of your oven and broil for about 5 minutes to brûlée the sugar.
15. Rest for a few minutes before serving with fresh berries.

CHOCOLATE DIPPED STRAWBERRIES

15 - 20 strawberries

15 – 20 ripe strawberries

12 ounces semi–sweet chocolate, chopped or discs

3 ounces milk or white chocolate, chopped or discs

OPTIONAL

2 – 4 ounces of Grand Marnier

SPECIAL EQUIPMENT: Injection Syringe

1. Rinse and thoroughly dry the strawberries; leave the stems on.
2. Line a sheet pan that will fit in your refrigerator with parchment paper.
3. Prepare a double boiler and place it over medium heat to melt the chocolate. Place 8 ounces of the semisweet chocolate in the double boiler and stir until completely melted.
4. Remove from heat before adding the remaining 4 ounces of chocolate, then stir until smooth and glossy. The chocolate should be warm but not hot for dipping, around 90° F. (See Tempering Chocolate tips on page 200.)
5. Prop a folded kitchen towel underneath one half of the chocolate pan so you have a deeper pool to dip from.
6. Holding the stem, dip each strawberry into the melted chocolate, exposing just a bit of the berry. Gently shake off the excess before placing it on the parchment-lined pan.
7. Refrigerate until the chocolate sets.
8. Melt the milk or white chocolate.
9. Fill the injection syringe with Grand Marnier.
10. Stick the needle in the exposed area of each strawberry and inject about 2 milliliters of Grand Marnier.
11. Use a fork to drizzle the milk or white chocolate over the strawberries.
12. Refrigerate until the chocolate has set before serving.

BREAD PUDDING WITH BOURBON CARAMEL SAUCE

8 - 10 servings

*6 cups Grandma's Rolls (page 25), cubed

2 cups milk

1 cup raisins

2 tablespoons dark rum

2 tablespoons bourbon

1 tablespoon brandy

2 tablespoons butter, softened

3 eggs

2 egg yolks

3/4 cup granulated sugar

1 1/2 cups heavy cream

ground or grated nutmeg

Bourbon Caramel Sauce

1/2 cup butter

1 1/2 cups brown sugar

1 cup heavy cream

1/4 cup bourbon

* Substitute any bakery-style white bread or rolls. It's best if they are a day or two old.

1. Soak the cubed rolls in the milk for 1 hour.
2. Separately, soak the raisins in the rum, bourbon, and brandy for 1 hour.
3. Preheat oven to 350º F.
4. Coat a 9x13-inch baking pan with soft butter.
5. Using a stand mixer with the wire whisk attachment or electric beaters, mix the eggs, egg yolks, and sugar until the mixture thickens and becomes light in color.
6. Add the heavy cream and whip until the cream thickens. Stir the raisins and alcohol into the egg, sugar, and cream mixture.
7. Gently fold the soaked bread into the cream mixture.
8. Pour the pudding into the buttered baking pan.
9. Sprinkle the top of the pudding with the ground or freshly grated nutmeg.
10. Place the pan in a slightly larger pan (a high-sided roasting pan works well) and fill it with lukewarm water, so it comes halfway up the pudding pan.
11. Bake in the water bath in the preheated oven for about 45 minutes.
12. While the pudding is baking, make the Bourbon Caramel Sauce.
13. In a medium-sized saucepan, melt the butter over medium heat.
14. Stir in the brown sugar, heavy cream, and bourbon.
15. Bring the sauce to a boil on medium-high heat and allow it to boil for 5 minutes. Adjust the heat to ensure it stays at a low boil, and stir occasionally.
16. Serve the pudding warm, topped with a generous spoonful or two of Caramel Sauce and Whipped Cream (page 198).

Pictured on page 196

CHOCOLATE DIPPED COCONUT MACAROONS

approximately 30 macaroons

5 cups sweetened shredded coconut

2 teaspoons vanilla extract

1/2 teaspoon salt

2/3 cup sweetened condensed milk

2 egg whites

12 ounces semi-sweet chocolate, chopped or discs

1. Preheat oven to 350º F.
2. Line a cookie sheet with parchment paper.
3. Place the coconut, vanilla, salt, and condensed milk in a mixing bowl. Stir until well combined.
4. Use electric beaters to whip the egg whites in a separate bowl until they can form soft peaks.
5. Gently fold the egg whites into the coconut batter until fully combined.
6. Drop large spoonfuls of batter, about two inches in diameter, onto the lined cookie sheet (a mini cookie scoop works well). Leave about two inches of space between each spoonful.
7. Bake for 10 - 12 minutes. The tops of the macaroons should be golden brown in color.
8. Allow them to cool completely before dipping them in chocolate.
9. Prepare a double boiler and place it over medium heat to melt the chocolate. Melt 8 ounces of chocolate in the top pan of the double boiler and stir until it is completely melted. Remove it from the heat.
10. Add the remaining 4 ounces of chocolate and stir until smooth and glossy. The chocolate should be warm but not hot, around 95º F. (See Tempering Chocolate tips on page 200.)
11. Prepare another sheet pan lined with parchment paper.
12. Prop a folded kitchen towel underneath one half of the chocolate pan so you have a deeper pool to dip from.
13. Dip each macaroon halfway into the melted chocolate, then lightly shake to remove excess chocolate.
14. Place the dipped macaroons on the fresh paper-lined pan.
15. Refrigerate until the chocolate has set before serving.

CAKES, FROSTINGS, & CHEESECAKES

Dark Chocolate Ganache 216

Chocolate Buttercream Frosting 217

Mom's Chocolate Cake 218

Chocolate Truffle Cake 220

Citrus Pound Cake with Oregon Berries 221

Carrot Cake 222

Lemon Cream Cheese Frosting 223

Grand Marnier Poppyseed Cake 224

Mocha Roulade 226

Hazelnut Cheesecake 228

Pumpkin Cheesecake 230

White Chocolate Cheesecake with Raspberry Sauce 232

Peanut Butter Cheesecake with Dark Chocolate Ganache 234

Chocolate Cheesecake 236

Me with my castle cake, 1974

When Billy was thirteen, he made the Enchanted Castle Cake from Betty Crocker's Cookbook for Boys and Girls on my fifth birthday. It was chocolate cake with vanilla frosting. The towers were made from sugar ice cream cones, the bricks from pillow mints, and the doors from chocolate bars. It lived up to its name; I was enchanted and delighted. Looking back, I realize what a sweet gesture it was from an adolescent kid to his baby sister. He made me another one a few years later and eventually made them for his daughters' birthdays. In a recent conversation, my niece was quite surprised to find out she was not the first recipient of the famous castle cake.

That castle cake was one of the first inspirations for my love of baking.

I also was a child deeply devoted to sugary sweets with a particular fondness for chocolate. Our mom rarely bought packaged cookies, candy, or cakes. With six kids, they didn't last long when she did. We knew that if we wanted sweets, we had better learn to bake them ourselves.

Mom was happy to teach us and kept the pantry stocked with flour, sugar, baking soda, cocoa powder, and vanilla. She was a great baker and preferred it to cooking, which she also did well but considered a chore. Her chocolate cake recipe was handed down to her by her mother, and it was the top choice for birthdays, picnics, and Sunday suppers. When I worked at the Treehouse, I received many requests for custom birthday cakes, and Mom's Chocolate Cake was the recipe I used. My decorating skills have never been impressive, but it won the award for Best Tasting Cake in the only contest I ever entered against other bakeries in Eugene. I don't recall the details, but the prize was two tickets to the Oregon Ducks football game, which made my husband, Bob, very happy. It's still the cake most requested by my family members, and my daughters, Hailey and Ella, have become quite skilled at making it. Hailey bakes the cake, and Ella makes the frosting. Their Grandma Betty would be so proud.

Cheesecake was a staple on the Treehouse dessert cart, and I chose my five favorite variations to include in this chapter, complete with instructions on how to bake them in a water bath. Few things impress dinner guests more than a cheesecake. You'll be met with protests like "but it's so rich" and "I really shouldn't," but trust me, it will magically disappear by the end of the evening.

A delicious cake is the ultimate celebration dessert, and I hope you find many occasions to use the following recipes to celebrate special people and events in your life.

DARK CHOCOLATE GANACHE

2 cups

10 ounces semisweet or bittersweet chocolate, chopped or discs

1 cup heavy cream

1 tablespoon butter, softened

pinch of salt

1 teaspoon vanilla or coffee extract

1. Place the chocolate in a heat-safe bowl.
2. Heat up the heavy cream in the microwave or on the stove. It should be hot enough to melt the chocolate but not boiling. Scrape off any "skin" that may have formed on top, then pour the cream over the top of the chocolate chips.

3. Stir with a wire whisk until all the chocolate has melted.
4. Add butter, salt, and vanilla or coffee extract. Stir until smooth.
5. Cool at room temperature or chill in the refrigerator to the desired consistency, depending on how it will be used.

Some of the many ways to use ganache:

* Mom's Chocolate Cake (page 218)
* Peanut Butter Cheesecake (page 234)
* Mudd Pie (page 254)
* Heat it to top ice cream or drizzle over fruit.
* Cool it until it's a spreadable filling.
* Cool, then whip it with electric beaters for a fluffy frosting.
* Add it to hot milk for decadent hot chocolate.
* Pipe it for cake decoration.
* Eat it right off the spoon.

CHOCOLATE BUTTERCREAM FROSTING

makes enough for a double layer cake or 24 cupcakes

1 1/2 cups butter, softened to room temp
1/3 cup unsweetened cocoa powder
1/4 teaspoon sea salt
1/4 cup milk, divided
2 teaspoons pure vanilla extract
6 cups powdered sugar, divided

1. Combine butter, cocoa, salt, 2 tablespoons of milk, vanilla, and 3 cups of powdered sugar in a large mixing bowl or the bowl of a stand mixer.
2. Beat well with electric beaters or a stand mixer fitted with a wire whisk until thoroughly combined. Scrape down the sides of the bowl with a rubber spatula as needed.
3. One cup at a time, add the remaining 3 cups of powdered sugar alternately with the remaining 2 tablespoons of milk until fully incorporated. The frosting should be quite thick at this point. Continue to beat well until it becomes fluffy and spreadable. Add a bit more milk if necessary.
4. Frost Mom's Chocolate Cake (page 218) or your favorite cupcakes.

MOM'S CHOCOLATE CAKE

8 - 12 servings

2 cups granulated sugar

1/2 cup butter, softened to room temp

1/4 cup canola or vegetable oil

3 eggs

1 teaspoon vanilla extract

1 cup buttermilk or 1 tablespoon vinegar + 1 cup (less 1 tablespoon) milk

2 cups all-purpose flour

2/3 cup unsweetened cocoa powder

2 teaspoons baking soda

3/4 teaspoon salt

1/2 cup hot water or brewed coffee

1 cup Dark Chocolate Ganache (page 216), cooled to a spreadable consistency

1 batch Chocolate Buttercream Frosting (page 217)

1. Preheat oven to 350º F.
2. Thoroughly coat two 9-inch round pans with cooking spray or line them with parchment paper. (If you use parchment paper, give the pans a light spray first to help it adhere.)
3. Beat the butter, oil, and sugar untl light and fluffy in a large mixing bowl or the bowl of a stand mixer.
4. Add eggs, one at a time, mix well after each addition.
5. Add vanilla extract.
6. Measure out buttermilk or combine the vinegar and milk. Microwave it for about 30 seconds or warm it on the stove to take the chill off and bring it to room temperature.
7. Sift the flour, cocoa powder, baking soda, and salt in a separate bowl.
8. Add one-third of the flour mixture to the butter mixture and mix until combined.
9. Add 1/2 of the buttermilk and mix until combined.
10. Repeat steps 8 and 9 until all the flour mixture and buttermilk are incorporated into the batter.
11. Mix in the hot water or coffee.
12. Pour the batter into the prepared pans, dividing it equally among them.
13. Bake for 25 to 30 minutes. A toothpick inserted in the center of the cake should come out clean.
14. Cool the cakes completely.
15. Fill the middle layer with Dark Chocolate Ganache and frost the top and sides with Chocolate Buttercream Frosting.

(Okay, Mom never actually used ganache, but she'd approve!)

The cake of our childhood

CHOCOLATE TRUFFLE CAKE

12 servings

1 tablespoon butter, soft or melted

2 tablespoons cocoa powder, sifted

Cake

1 pound semi-sweet chocolate, chopped or discs

3/4 cup butter

1 teaspoon vanilla extract

1/2 teaspoon coffee extract

1/2 teaspoon sea salt

5 eggs, separated

2 tablespoons granulated sugar

Topping

Whipped Cream (page 198)

Raspberry Sauce (page 199)

1. Preheat oven to 325° F.
2. Line a 9-inch cake pan with parchment paper or foil. Make sure it overlaps a bit; you will use it to lift the cake from the pan.
3. Coat the bottom and sides of the lined pan with the butter, then sift in the cocoa powder to coat the pan, tapping out the excess cocoa.
4. Set up a double boiler, making sure the top pan is over, not in, the water.
5. Place the chocolate and butter in the top pan and melt over medium heat, stirring until smooth. Turn the heat to low or off and keep the mixture warm, but not hot, while you prepare the eggs.
6. Separate the egg yolks and whites into two separate mixing bowls.
7. Beat the yolks until they are thick and pale yellow.
8. Beat the whites until soft peaks form; add the sugar and beat until stiff peaks form.
9. Pour the chocolate mixture into a large mixing bowl and stir in the vanilla extract, coffee extract, and salt.
10. Gently fold the egg yolks into the chocolate mixture until combined, then gently fold in the egg whites until fully combined. Do not overmix or the batter will deflate.
11. Spread the batter into the prepared pan.
12. Bake on the middle rack of the preheated oven for 20 - 25 minutes. It should be risen but still loose in the center when gently shaken. A slight crack on top is okay.
13. Allow the cake to cool for 30 minutes, then refrigerate until it's cooled and set.
14. Slice with a hot knife and serve with raspberry sauce and whipped cream.

See Tips for Separating Eggs on page 85

CITRUS POUND CAKE

6 - 8 servings

1/2 cup butter, softened to room temp

3/4 cup granulated sugar

2 eggs

1 cup flour, sifted

1/4 tsp salt

2 teaspoons orange juice

2 teaspoons vanilla extract

1 teaspoon lemon zest

TOPPING

2 cups fresh berries

1 tablespoon granulated sugar

1 tablespoon fresh lemon juice

1 tablespoon powdered sugar

whipped cream (page 198)

mint leaves (optional)

1. Preheat oven to 325° F.
2. Coat one 9-inch round cake pan with cooking spray.
3. Beat butter and sugar in a large mixing bowl or the bowl of a stand mixer until the mixture is light and fluffy.
4. Add eggs, one at a time, and mix well after each addition.
5. Add flour and salt; mix well.
6. Add orange juice, vanilla extract, and lemon zest; mix well.
7. Spread the batter evenly into the prepared pan.
8. Bake for about 30 minutes. The cake should be golden on top and a toothpick inserted in the center should come out clean.
9. Remove the cake from the pan onto a cooling rack or parchment-lined plate. Let it cool and prepare the berries.
10. Place the berries in a large bowl and add sugar and lemon juice. Let them sit for 20 -30 minutes, so they form a light syrup to soak into the cake.
11. Sift powdered sugar over the top of the cake and cut it into wedges.
12. Serve individual slices with the berries and whipped cream. Garnish with mint leaves.

Double the recipe and freeze a cake. Thaw it for a quick dessert when your favorite berries are in season.

CARROT CAKE

12 - 16 servings

2 cups granulated sugar

1 1/2 cups canola or vegetable oil

4 eggs

1 teaspoon vanilla extract

2 cups all-purpose flour

1 teaspoon baking soda

1 teaspoon salt

2 tablespoons ground cinnamon

4 cups grated carrots
(about 10 medium-sized carrots)

1 cup shredded unsweetened coconut

*1 1/2 cups raisins, soaked and drained

Lemon Cream Cheese Frosting
(page 223)

1 cup toasted pecans, chopped

* Cover the raisins with hot tap water and allow them to soak for at least fifteen minutes. Drain before adding them to the cake batter.

1. Preheat oven to 350º F.
2. Thoroughly coat two 9-inch round pans with cooking spray or line them with parchment paper. (If you use parchment paper, give the pans a light spray first to help it adhere.)
3. Scrub or peel the carrots and trim the ends. Grate them in a food processor or a box grater to yield 4 cups.
4. Place the sugar and oil in a large mixing bowl or the bowl of a stand mixer and beat until well combined.
5. Add eggs, one at a time, mixing well after each addition. Add vanilla extract.
6. Whisk the flour, baking soda, salt, and cinnamon together in a separate bowl.
7. Add the flour mixture to the sugar mixture and mix well.
8. Mix in the carrots, coconut, and raisins.
9. Pour the batter evenly into the prepared pans.
10. Bake for 35 - 40 minutes. A toothpick inserted in the center of the cake should come out clean.
11. Allow the cakes to cool completely before frosting. (I stick them in the fridge, so they are cold and easier to cut into halves.)
12. Cut the cooled cakes in half horizontally.
13. Frost each layer, the top, and sides with Lemon Cream Cheese Frosting.
14. Press the toasted pecans into the frosting on the side of the cake and along the top edge.
15. Keep refrigerated before and between servings.

LEMON CREAM CHEESE FROSTING

24 ounces cream cheese, softened to room temp

1 cup butter, softened to room temp

2 tablespoons lemon juice

1 teaspoon vanilla

3 cups powdered sugar

1. Beat the softened cream cheese in a large mixing bowl or the bowl of a stand mixer on medium-high speed, scraping sides occasionally until it is completely smooth.

2. Gradually add the butter and beat until the mixture is completely smooth. (Both the cream cheese and the butter must be softened to room temperature to properly blend together.)

3. Add lemon juice and vanilla extract.

4. On low speed, add the powdered sugar 1 cup at a time.

5. Once the powdered sugar is fully incorporated, increase the speed and mix until the frosting is smooth and fluffy.

GRAND MARNIER POPPYSEED CAKE

12 - 16 servings

1 1/2 cups granulated sugar

1/2 cup butter, softened to room temp

1/2 cup canola or vegetable oil

2 eggs

4 egg whites

1 teaspoon pure vanilla extract

2 tablespoons orange juice

2 2/3 cups all-purpose flour

2 tablespoons cornstarch

1 tablespoon baking powder

1 teaspoon sea salt

1/2 cup milk

1/3 cup poppyseeds

GRAND MARNIER BUTTERCREAM

1 1/4 cups granulated sugar

5 egg whites

2 cups butter, softened to room temp

1 teaspoon vanilla extract

1 tablespoon Grand Marnier (orange brandy liqueur)

1/3 cup Grand Marnier (for soaking the cake)

1. Preheat oven to 350º F.
2. Thoroughly coat two 9-inch round pans with cooking spray or line them with parchment paper. (If you use parchment paper, give the pans a light spray first to help it adhere.)
3. Beat the sugar, butter, and oil in a large mixing bowl or the bowl of a stand mixer until light and fluffy.
4. Add the eggs, one at a time, and the egg whites, beating well after each addition.
5. Mix in the vanilla and orange juice.
6. Sift the flour, cornstarch, baking powder, and salt into a separate bowl.
7. Add one-third of the flour mixture to the butter mixture and mix until combined.
8. Add 1/4 cup milk and mix until combined.
9. Repeat steps 7 and 8 until all of the flour mixture and milk are incorporated.
10. Stir in the poppy seeds.
11. Pour the batter evenly into the prepared pans.
12. Bake for 25 to 30 minutes. A toothpick inserted in the center of the cake should come out clean.
13. Cool the cakes while you make the buttercream.

BUTTERCREAM

14. Fill a saucepan halfway with water and set it over medium-high heat to simmer.
15. Mix the sugar and egg whites with a wire whisk in a large, heatproof mixing bowl. The stainless steel bowl of a stand mixer works well, or heatproof glass.
16. Place the bowl over the simmering water and whisk constantly until the sugar has dissolved and the temperature reaches 160º F on an instant-read or candy thermometer. (If you don't have a thermometer, test it with a spoon to ensure it is hot and the sugar has dissolved.)
17. Remove the mixture from the heat and beat with the whisk attachment of a stand mixer or electric beaters until it can form stiff peaks.

An elegant cake with a silky Swiss buttercream

18. Gradually add the soft butter, a few tablespoons at a time, mixing thoroughly after each addition.

19. Add the vanilla and liqueur. The buttercream should be thick and silky smooth.

ASSEMBLE

20. Cut each cake in half horizontally.

21. Use a pastry brush to soak the first layer with 1/3 of the liqueur and spread it with a layer of buttercream. Repeat with two more layers.

22. Frost the top and sides of the cake with the remaining buttercream. Garnish as desired.

23. Keep refrigerated but take it out about 30 minutes before serving to take the chill off.

MOCHA ROULADE

12 servings

Sponge

6 eggs at room temperature, separated (See tips on page 85)

3/4 cup granulated sugar, divided

1 teaspoon vanilla extract

1/4 teaspoon salt

1/3 cup cocoa powder

1/3 cup all-purpose flour

Glaze

8 ounces semisweet chocolate, chopped or discs

4 ounces strong brewed coffee

Cream Filling

2 cups heavy cream

1/4 cup coffee liqueur

powdered sugar for dusting

1. Preheat oven to 400° F.
2. Spray a half-sheet pan (18" x 13" x 1") with cooking spray, then line it with parchment paper so that it comes up the sides of the pan. Spray or butter the parchment paper and set the pan aside.
3. Separate the egg yolks from the whites into two large mixing bowls.
4. Beat the yolks with an electric mixer until they are thick and pale yellow.
5. Beat 1/2 cup of the sugar, vanilla, and salt into the yolks.
6. Sift the cocoa powder and flour over the yolk mixture and stir it in.
7. Clean the beaters, then whip the egg whites until soft peaks form. Add 1/4 cup sugar and beat until stiff peaks form.
8. Stir one-quarter of the egg white mixture into the yolk mixture to loosen it a bit, then gently fold in the remaining egg whites until combined. Do not overmix, or you will deflate the batter.
9. Spread the batter evenly into the prepared pan.
10. Bake for 9 - 11 minutes. The cake should be puffy and spring back when touched, but be careful not to overbake. It will deflate a bit upon removal from the oven.
11. Allow the cake to cool for about five minutes, then dust the top thoroughly with powdered sugar.
12. Place a large sheet of parchment paper on a cutting board as large as the pan or the back of another half-sheet pan. Place it, parchment side down, over the cake and quickly flip it over, so it is powdered sugar-side down on the clean parchment.
13. Gently remove the parchment in which it was baked and allow the cake to cool while you make the glaze and cream filling.
14. Stir the hot coffee into the semi-sweet chocolate and whisk until the chocolate is melted and shiny. If necessary, heat the mixture in the microwave for 15 - 30 seconds to completely melt the chocolate.
15. Spread the glaze evenly over the cake.
16. Whip the cream until it becomes thick enough to hold its shape, then add the coffee liqueur.
17. Carefully spread the cream over the glaze on the cake; try to avoid swirling the two together.
18. Use the parchment paper to gently roll the cake into about a 3-inch high roll. Place it seam-side down and refrigerate for at least an hour.
19. Dust the top of the rolled cake with powdered sugar.
20. Use a hot knife to cut it into slices. Cut the ends at an angle for a nice presentation, so they show off the roll. (Keep the rough ends for yourself to snack on!)

HAZELNUT CHEESECAKE

16 servings (Plan to make one day ahead to allow the cheesecake to be fully set.)

Special equipment: 9-inch Springform pan and a large, high-sided roasting pan for the water bath.

CRUST

2 cups finely ground graham crackers
(14 whole crackers)

1/2 cup butter, melted

FILLING

2 pounds cream cheese, softened to room temp

1 1/2 cups granulated sugar

3 eggs

1/3 cup sour cream

1/4 cup hazelnut liqueur

1 1/2 cups whole hazelnuts, roasted and ground
(see page 56)

SOUR CREAM TOPPING

8 ounces cream cheese, softened to room temp

2-4 tablespoons powdered sugar

1/3 cup sour cream

1 teaspoon vanilla extract

GARNISH

1/2 cup roasted hazelnuts, roughly chopped

1. Preheat oven to 350º F.
2. Line a 9-inch springform pan tightly with foil, making sure there are no punctures, to prevent water from getting in when the cheesecake bakes in the water bath.
3. Place the graham crackers in the bowl of a food processor or blender and pulse to a crumb texture. Add the melted butter and pulse until well combined.
4. Transfer the graham cracker mixture to the prepared spring-form pan and press down to form a crust on the bottom of the pan.
5. Bake in the preheated oven for 10 minutes, then set aside to cool while you make the filling. Leave the oven on.
6. Whip the cream cheese in a large mixing bowl or a stand mixer bowl until it is completely smooth, frequently scraping the sides of the bowl.
7. Grind the hazelnuts in a food processor or blender.
8. Gradually add sugar, eggs, sour cream, hazelnut liqueur, and ground hazelnuts to the cream cheese, beating well and scraping sides after each addition until thoroughly combined.
9. Pour the batter over the crust into the springform pan.

Oregon's Willamette Valley produces the majority of hazelnuts, also known as filberts, in the USA

10. Prepare a water bath in a baking pan a little larger than the springform (a turkey roaster works nicely). Place the springform inside of it, and fill it with lukewarm tap water to reach halfway up the side of the springform pan. This will create steam and prevent it from drying and cracking in the oven.

11. Bake for 1 1/2 - 2 hours. The top should be slightly risen and golden brown.

12. Remove the cheesecake from the water bath and allow it to cool for about 30 minutes, then refrigerate for at least 6 hours to ensure it's fully set.

13. For the topping: Whip the cream cheese with the powdered sugar until it is completely smooth.

14. Add sour cream and vanilla; mix well.

15. Remove the chilled cheesecake from the spring-form pan and foil and set it on a serving plate or small cutting board.

16. Spread the topping evenly on the cheesecake and garnish with hazelnuts.

17. Use a sharp knife dipped in hot water to cut the cheesecake, and have a cloth handy to wipe off the excess. For best results, cut it in half first, then quarters, and so on to make the slices uniform.

18. Keep refrigerated between servings.

PUMPKIN CHEESECAKE

16 servings (Plan to make one day ahead to allow the cheesecake to be fully set.)

Special equipment: 9-inch Springform pan and a large, high-sided roasting pan for the water bath.

CRUST

1 1/2 cups ground graham crackers
(12 whole crackers)

1/2 cup pecans or gingersnaps
(substitute with more graham crackers)

1/2 cup butter, melted

FILLING

2 pounds cream cheese, softened to room temp

1 1/2 cups granulated sugar

3 eggs

1/3 cup sour cream

15 ounces canned pumpkin

1 teaspoon vanilla extract

1 teaspoon cinnamon

1/2 teaspoon ground ginger

1/2 teaspoon ground nutmeg

TOPPING

Whipped Cream (page 218)

ground cinnamon or grated nutmeg

1. Preheat oven to 350º F.
2. Line a 9-inch springform pan tightly with foil, making sure there are no punctures, to prevent water from getting in when the cheesecake bakes in the water bath.
3. Place the graham crackers with the pecans or gingersnaps in the bowl of a food processor or blender and pulse to a crumb texture. Add the melted butter and pulse until well combined.
4. Transfer the graham cracker mixture to the prepared spring-form pan and press down to form a crust on the bottom of the pan.
5. Bake in the preheated oven for 10 minutes, then set aside to cool while you make the filling. Leave the oven on.
6. Whip the cream cheese in a large mixing bowl or a stand mixer bowl until it is completely smooth, frequently scraping the sides of the bowl.
7. Gradually add sugar, eggs, sour cream, pumpkin, vanilla, cinnamon, ginger, and nutmeg to the cream cheese, beating well and scraping sides after each addition until thoroughly combined.
8. Pour the batter over the crust into the springform pan.
9. Prepare a water bath in a baking pan a little larger than the springform (a turkey roaster works nicely). Place the springform inside of it, and fill it with lukewarm tap water to reach halfway up the side of the springform pan. This will create steam and prevent it from drying and cracking in the oven.
10. Bake for 1 1/2 - 2 hours. The top should be slightly risen and golden brown.
11. Remove the cheesecake from the water bath and allow it to cool for about 30 minutes, then refrigerate for at least 6 hours to ensure it's fully set.
12. Remove the chilled cheesecake from the spring-form pan and foil and set it on a serving plate or small cutting board.
13. Use a sharp knife dipped in hot water to cut the cheesecake, and have a cloth handy to wipe off the excess. For best results, cut it in half first, then quarters, and so on to make the slices uniform.
14. Keep refrigerated between servings.

Top each slice with whipped cream and a dusting of cinnamon or nutmeg

WHITE CHOCOLATE CHEESECAKE WITH RASPBERRY SAUCE

16 servings (Plan to make one day ahead to allow the cheesecake to be fully set.)

Special equipment: 9-inch Springform pan and a large, high-sided roasting pan for the water bath.

CRUST

20 chocolate sandwich cookies

1/4 cup butter, melted

FILLING

2 pounds cream cheese, softened to room temp

1 1/2 cups granulated sugar

3 eggs

10 ounces white chocolate, chopped or discs

5 tablespoons heavy cream

1/2 cup sour cream

1/4 cup Grand Marnier or triple sec liqueur

TOPPING

Raspberry Sauce (page 199)

Whipped Cream (page 198)

fresh raspberries

1. Preheat oven to 350º F.
2. Line a 9-inch springform pan tightly with foil, making sure there are no punctures, to prevent water from getting in when the cheesecake bakes in the water bath.
3. Place the cookies in the bowl of a food processor or blender and pulse to a crumb texture. Add the melted butter and pulse until well combined.
4. Transfer the cookie mixture to the prepared spring-form pan and press down to form a crust on the bottom of the pan.
5. Bake in the preheated oven for 10 minutes, then set aside to cool while you make the filling. Leave the oven on.
6. Whip the cream cheese in a large mixing bowl or a stand mixer bowl until it is completely smooth, frequently scraping the sides of the bowl.
7. Melt 6 ounces of the white chocolate in the microwave or a double boiler. Remove it from the heat, add the remaining 4 ounces of white chocolate, and stir until it's completely melted. It should be lukewarm when you add it to the batter.
8. Gradually add sugar, eggs, melted white chocolate, heavy cream, sour cream, and liqueur to the cream cheese, beating well and scraping sides after each addition until thoroughly combined.
9. Pour the batter over the crust into the springform pan.
10. Prepare a water bath in a baking pan a little larger than the springform (a turkey roaster works nicely). Place the springform inside of it, and fill it with lukewarm tap water to reach halfway up the side of the springform pan. This will create steam and prevent it from drying and cracking in the oven.
11. Bake for 1 1/2 - 2 hours. The top should be slightly risen and golden brown.

12. Remove the cheesecake from the water bath and allow it to cool for about 30 minutes, then refrigerate for at least 6 hours to ensure it's fully set.
13. Remove the chilled cheesecake from the spring-form pan and foil and set it on a serving plate or small cutting board.
14. Use a sharp knife dipped in hot water to cut the cheesecake, and have a cloth handy to wipe off the excess. For best results, cut it in half first, then quarters, and so on to make the slices uniform.
15. Keep refrigerated between servings.
16. Serve each slice over a pool of raspberry sauce and top with whipped cream. Garnish with fresh raspberries.

PEANUT BUTTER CHEESECAKE WITH CHOCOLATE GANACHE

16 servings (Plan to make one day ahead to allow the cheesecake to be fully set.)

Special equipment: 9-inch Springform pan and a large, high-sided roasting pan for the water bath.

CRUST

20 chocolate sandwich cookies

1/4 cup butter, melted

FILLING

2 pounds cream cheese, softened to room temp

1 1/2 cups granulated sugar

3 eggs

1/2 cup sour cream

1 cup creamy peanut butter

1 teaspoon vanilla extract

TOPPING

2 cups Dark Chocolate Ganache (page 216)

3/4 cup roasted, salted peanuts, chopped

1. Preheat oven to 350º F.
2. Line a 9-inch springform pan tightly with foil, making sure there are no punctures, to prevent water from getting in when the cheesecake bakes in the water bath.
3. Place the cookies in the bowl of a food processor or blender and pulse to a crumb texture. Add the melted butter and pulse until well combined.
4. Transfer the cookie mixture to the prepared spring-form pan and press down to form a crust on the bottom of the pan.
5. Bake in the preheated oven for 10 minutes, then set aside to cool while you make the filling. Leave the oven on.
6. Whip the cream cheese in a large mixing bowl or a stand mixer bowl until it is completely smooth, frequently scraping the sides of the bowl.
7. Gradually add sugar, eggs, sour cream, peanut butter, and vanilla to the cream cheese, beating well and scraping sides after each addition until thoroughly combined.
8. Pour the batter over the crust into the springform pan.
9. Prepare a water bath in a baking pan a little larger than the springform (a turkey roaster works nicely). Place the springform inside of it, and fill it with lukewarm tap water to reach halfway up the side of the springform pan. This will create steam and prevent it from drying and cracking in the oven.
10. Bake for 1 1/2 - 2 hours. The top should be slightly risen and golden brown.
11. Remove the cheesecake from the water bath and allow it to cool for about 30 minutes, then refrigerate for at least 6 hours to ensure it's fully set.
12. Make the Dark Chocolate Ganache. It should be a pudding-like consistency, spreadable but not hardened. You may make it ahead of time, chill it, then warm it to the desired consistency, or make it once the cheesecake has fully set.
13. Remove the chilled cheesecake from the spring-form pan and foil, and set it on a serving plate or small cutting board.

14. Spread the ganache all over the top and sides of the cheesecake. It will begin to firm up as you work.

15. Sprinkle the peanuts on the top edge and gently press them into the ganache.

16. Chill for at least 30 minutes to set the ganache.

17. Use a sharp knife dipped in hot water to cut the cheesecake, and have a cloth handy to wipe off the excess cheesecake. For best results, cut it in half first, then quarters, and so on to make the slices uniform.

18. Keep refrigerated between servings.

CHOCOLATE CHEESECAKE

16 servings (Plan to make one day ahead to allow the cheesecake to be fully set.)

Special equipment: 9-inch Springform pan and a large, high-sided roasting pan for the water bath.

Crust

20 chocolate sandwich cookies

1/4 cup butter, melted

Filling

2 pounds cream cheese, softened to room temp

1 1/2 cups granulated sugar

3 eggs

10 ounces semisweet chocolate, chopped or discs

5 tablespoons heavy cream

1/2 cup sour cream

2 tablespoons strong cold coffee + 1 tablespoon vanilla extract or 1/4 cup coffee liqueur

Sour Cream Topping

8 ounces cream cheese, softened to room temp

2-4 tablespoons powdered sugar

1/3 cup sour cream

1 teaspoon vanilla extract

Garnish

1/3 cup chopped or shaved semisweet chocolate

1. Preheat oven to 350° F.
2. Line a 9-inch springform pan tightly with foil, making sure there are no punctures, to prevent water from getting in when the cheesecake bakes in the water bath.
3. Place the cookies in the bowl of a food processor or blender and pulse to a crumb texture. Add the melted butter and pulse until well combined.
4. Transfer the cookie mixture to the prepared spring-form pan and press down to form a crust on the bottom of the pan.
5. Bake in the preheated oven for 10 minutes, then set aside to cool while you make the filling. Leave the oven on.
6. Whip the cream cheese in a large mixing bowl or a stand mixer bowl until it is completely smooth, frequently scraping the sides of the bowl.
7. Melt 6 ounces of the semisweet chocoate in the microwave or a double boiler. Remove it from the heat, add the remaining 4 ounces of semisweet chocolate, and stir until it's completely melted. It should be lukewarm when you add it to the batter.
8. Gradually add sugar, eggs, melted chocolate, heavy cream, sour cream, coffee, and vanilla (substitute the coffee and vanilla with coffee liqueur if desired) to the cream cheese, beating well and scraping sides after each addition until thoroughly combined.
9. Pour the batter over the crust into the springform pan.
10. Prepare a water bath in a baking pan a little larger than the springform (a turkey roaster works nicely). Place the springform inside of it, and fill it with lukewarm tap water to reach halfway up the side of the springform pan. This will create steam and prevent it from drying and cracking in the oven.
11. Bake for 1 1/2 - 2 hours. The top should be slightly risen and brown.

12. Remove the cheesecake from the water bath and allow it to cool for about 30 minutes, then refrigerate for at least 6 hours to ensure it's fully set.

13. For the topping: Whip the cream cheese with the powdered sugar until it is completely smooth.

14. Add sour cream and vanilla; mix well.

15. Remove the chilled cheesecake from the spring-form pan and foil and set it on a serving plate or small cutting board.

16. Spread the topping evenly on the cheesecake. Garnish with shaved or chopped chocolate.

17. Use a sharp knife dipped in hot water to cut the cheesecake, and have a cloth handy to wipe off the excess. For best results, cut it in half first, then quarters, and so on to make the slices uniform.

18. Keep refrigerated between servings.

PIES & TURNOVERS

Rich Butter Pie Crust 242

Banana Cream Pie 244

Chocolate Cream Pie 246

Toasted Coconut Cream Pie 248

Bourbon Pecan Pie with Dark Chocolate 250

Fresh Berry Turnovers 253

Treehouse Mud Pie 254

Cousins at Grandma Betty's house
Thanksgiving 1995
Back: Steven, John
Front: Alicia, Nicole, Abigail

I'm a little obsessed with making the perfect pie crust.

It's my claim to fame on Thanksgiving Day and the only time I get the satisfaction of my brother Billy's three kids asking him why he can't make something as well as Aunt Molly. Given all the other accolades he receives, he doesn't take it as well as he should, but such is a chef's ego. I probably am not as gracious about it as I could be either, but such is the nature of little sisters.

Don't get me wrong, his pies are wonderful, and his Banana Cream Pie was a favorite among his customers at Billy Mac's. It really just comes down to the fact that, as a home cook and baker who is not a busy chef, I've had a lot more time over the years to concentrate on making the flakiest, best-tasting pie crust for my cream pies. I've found that using the best quality butter you can buy, keeping all the ingredients very cold, and adding a little apple cider vinegar are key elements to keep the compliments coming.

I'll show you how in my recipe for Rich Butter Pie Crust.

You will also find instructions to make delicious cream fillings for Dark Chocolate Cream Pie and Toasted Coconut Cream Pie, along with the decadent Bourbon Pecan Pie that's filled with chunks of semi-sweet chocolate.

On warm summer days when you don't want to be in the kitchen long, you can showcase fresh summer berries using frozen puff pastry. It's a shortcut I used at the Treehouse when I made Fresh Berry Turnovers with whatever the produce truck delivered in June through September; blueberries, blackberries, raspberries, and marionberries were often on board. The waitstaff topped the warm tarts with a scoop of vanilla ice cream before serving them to delighted customers.

Due to its generous size, the frozen Mudd Pie was often ordered as a shared dessert at the restaurant. The towering slab of coffee ice cream, chocolate ganache, and toasted almonds is a real crowd-pleaser.

Also, the chocolate cookie crust is so easy, you won't need to worry about any competitive siblings making it better than you.

RICH BUTTER PIE CRUST

makes two 9-inch crusts

1 cup butter, cold

3 cups all-purpose flour

1/2 teaspoon salt

2 tablespoons granulated sugar (omit for a savory pie or quiche)

1/2 cup water

1 teaspoon apple cider vinegar

ice

Egg Wash

1 egg

2 tablespoons water

1. Blend flour, sugar, and salt in a food processor.
2. Chop half of the cold butter into small chunks. Add it to the flour mixture and pulse until a coarse meal forms. (If you don't have a food processor, you can do it the old-fashioned way and use a manual pastry cutter or fork. It works well; in fact, it may yield an even flakier crust. It just requires more effort.)
3. Pour the water and apple cider vinegar over a cup of ice. Set aside.
4. Make sure all the flour is blended well with the butter. Loose flour will turn to paste once the water is added. Paste is not flaky. Chop and add the remaining butter and pulse until mostly combined. Some pea-size pieces of butter are desirable at this stage. They will create little pockets of steam and add to the flakiness. Loose flour = tough pastry. Loose butter = flaky pastry.
5. Add the water and vinegar (strained from the ice) and pulse until the dough begins to come together. Moist clumps should form. If the dough is too dry, add a little more ice water.
6. Place a large sheet of plastic wrap on the countertop or another work surface. Transfer the dough onto it and, using your hands, gather the dough together and cut it in half. Form the dough into two disks, and wrap them separately in plastic wrap. Refrigerate for at least 1 hour and up to a few days. Freeze for up to three months.
7. Remove the dough from the refrigerator 15 minutes before you roll it out or for at least one hour from the freezer.
8. Dust a flat work surface with flour. Begin to roll out the dough with a wooden or marble rolling pin. Roll it a little one way, turn it 90 degrees, and roll more. Turn it over and repeat until it is about 6 inches larger in diameter than the pie plate, adding flour as needed. If it breaks a little, press it back together and continue.
9. Carefully fold the dough in half, lift it onto the pie plate, and unfold it, so it overlaps the rim of the pie plate. Fold the dough edge under to have a uniform overlap of about 1 inch. Trim excess dough as needed. Use your thumb and two index fingers to make a fluted edge.
10. Chill for at least 30 minutes before baking.

Excess pie dough cut into strips, brushed with egg wash, and baked with cinnamon and sugar.

Parbaking and Baking the Crust

1. Preheat oven to 375º F.

2. Line the chilled crust with parchment paper or aluminum foil and fill the bottom with pie weights or dried beans. Be careful not to press the parchment paper or foil into the crust, but it should rest against it to keep the sides from sinking.

3. Bake for 25 - 30 minutes until the sides are set and pale golden.

4. Whisk the egg and water together to make the egg wash.

5. For a parbaked crust, used with pies that need further baking, like fruit pies, quiche, etc.: Remove the crust from the oven and brush the entire crust with egg wash. Allow the crust to cool. Fill it with the desired filling and bake according to the recipe you use. I recommend you cover the edge of the crust with a silicon pie crust ring or make a ring with aluminum foil to prevent burning while the filling bakes.

6. For a fully baked crust, used with custard and cream pies that don't require more baking after they are filled: Remove the crust from the oven and remove the foil and pie weights. Prick the bottom of the crust with a fork to prevent puffing, and brush the entire crust with egg wash. Return it to the oven and bake for another 5-10 minutes until golden brown. Allow it to cool before filling.

An egg wash creates a barrier between the crust and the filling, preventing a soggy crust

BANANA CREAM PIE

makes one 9-inch pie, about 8 servings

one 9-inch pie crust, baked
(try Rich Butter Pie Crust page 242)

2 large bananas, sliced

Custard

3 cups milk, 2% or whole

4 egg yolks

3/4 cup granulated sugar

1/3 cup flour

1/2 teaspoon sea salt

2 tablespoons butter

1 tablespoon vanilla extract

Topping

one large banana, sliced

Whipped Cream (page 198)

caramel or chocolate sauce (optional)

1. Bake the pie crust and allow it to cool.

2. Slice the bananas and place them in an even layer in the cooled crust.

3. Heat the milk in the microwave for 2 minutes to take the chill off and speed up the cooking process.

4. Separate the egg yolks into a medium-sized mixing bowl and set aside. Reserve the whites for another use.

5. Gather the remaining ingredients for the custard and place them near the stove for easy access.

6. Whisk together the sugar, flour, and salt in a large saucepan until combined.

7. Add 1/2 cup of milk at a time and whisk it in with the flour mixture until completely smooth before adding the next 1/2 cup, then repeat until all of the milk is added.

8. Once you have at least half the milk added, place the pan on the stove over medium heat and cook until the mixture comes to a low simmer and starts to thicken. Stir frequently with a wire whisk, scraping the bottom and sides of the pan to keep an even texture. This should take about ten minutes.

9. Once the mixture has thickened to a texture similar to heavy cream, it's time to temper the yolks.

10. Begin by whisking the yolks in the mixing bowl so they are broken and well combined. Very slowly add 1/2 cup of the hot milk mixture and briskly whisk it into the yolks. Repeat until you have added about 2 cups of the hot mixture. Whisking constantly, pour the tempered yolk mixture into the saucepan and stir until well combined.

11. Stir constantly over medium heat and bring the custard to a low boil.

12. Cook for five minutes, stirring often until it thickens to a warm pudding consistency. Test it by coating a spoon; you should be able to run a finger through it without it running. Remove the custard from the heat.

13. Use a fine mesh strainer to strain it into a large mixing bowl to remove any lumps.

14. Add the butter and vanilla extract and stir until the custard is smooth.

15. Pour the custard in an even layer over the bananas.

Try it with a drizzle of Bourbon Caramel Sauce (page 210) or warm Dark Chocolate Ganache, (page 216)

16. Cover the pie with plastic wrap and chill in the refrigerator until it is set, at least 4 hours and up to 24 hours.

17. Garnish the pie with fresh banana slices, whipped cream, and a drizzle of caramel or chocolate sauce.

DARK CHOCOLATE CREAM PIE

makes one 9-inch pie, about 8 servings

one 9-inch pie crust, baked
(try Rich Butter Pie Crust page 242)

Custard

3 cups milk, 2% or whole

1/2 cup granulated sugar

1/3 cup all-purpose flour

1/2 teaspoon sea salt

3 egg yolks

2 oz unsweetened chocolate, chopped

4oz semi-sweet chocolate, chopped

2 tablespoons butter

2 teaspoons vanilla or 1 teaspoon coffee extract

Topping

Whipped Cream (page 198)

1/3 cup shaved or chopped chocolate

1. Bake the pie crust and allow it to cool.

2. Heat the milk in the microwave for 2 minutes to take the chill off and speed up the cooking process.

3. Separate the egg yolks into a medium-sized mixing bowl and set aside. Reserve the whites for another use.

4. Gather the remaining ingredients for the custard and place them near the stove for easy access.

5. Whisk together the sugar, flour, and salt in a large saucepan until combined.

6. Add 1/2 cup of milk at a time and whisk it in with the flour mixture until completely smooth before adding the next 1/2 cup, then repeat until all of the milk is added.

7. Once you have at least half the milk added, place the pan on the stove over medium heat and cook until the mixture comes to a low simmer and starts to thicken. Stir frequently with a wire whisk, scraping the bottom and sides of the pan to keep an even texture. This should take about ten minutes.

8. Once the mixture has thickened to a texture similar to heavy cream, it's time to temper the yolks.

9. Begin by whisking the yolks in the mixing bowl so they are broken and well combined. Slowly add 1/2 cup of the hot milk mixture and briskly whisk it into the yolks. Repeat until you have added about 2 cups of the hot mixture. Whisking constantly, pour the tempered yolk mixture into the saucepan and stir until well combined.

10. Stir constantly over medium heat and bring the custard to a low boil.

11. Cook for five minutes, stirring often until it thickens to a warm pudding consistency. Test it by coating a spoon; you should be able to run a finger through it without it running. Remove the custard from the heat.

12. Place the chopped unsweetened chocolate, semisweet chocolate, butter, and vanilla or coffee extract in a large mixing bowl.

13. Use a fine mesh strainer and strain the custard into the bowl with the chocolate and stir until the custard is smooth.

14. Pour the custard into the pie crust.

15. Cover the pie with plastic wrap and chill in the refrigerator until it is set, at least 4 hours and up to 24 hours.

16. Serve with whipped cream and shaved or chopped chocolate.

Use a vegetable peeler on a block of chocolate to make cute little curls

TOASTED COCONUT CREAM PIE

makes one 9-inch pie, about 8 servings

one 9-inch pie crust, baked
(try Rich Butter Pie Crust page 242)

FILLING

3 cups unsweetened coconut milk

3/4 cup Toasted Coconut (opposite page)

1/2 cup all-purpose flour

3/4 cup granulated sugar

1/2 teaspoon sea salt

4 egg yolks

2 tablespoons butter

1 tablespoon pure vanilla extract

TOPPING

Whipped Cream (page 198)

3/4 cup Toasted Coconut (opposite page)

1. Bake the pie crust and allow it to cool.
2. Heat the coconut milk in the microwave or on the stove until it is hot but not boiling.
3. Add the toasted coconut and steep it in the hot milk for 30 minutes. Strain the coconut out of the milk and discard or reserve for another purpose.
4. Separate the egg yolks into a medium-sized mixing bowl and set aside. Reserve the whites for another use.
5. Whisk together the sugar, flour, and salt in a large saucepan until combined.
6. Add 1/2 cup of coconut milk at a time to the saucepan and whisk it in with the flour mixture until completely smooth before adding the next 1/2 cup, then repeat until all of the milk is added.
7. Once you have at least half the milk added, place the pan on the stove over medium heat and cook until the mixture comes to a low simmer and starts to thicken. Stir frequently with a wire whisk, scraping the bottom and sides of the pan to keep an even texture. This should take about ten minutes.
8. Once the mixture has thickened to a texture similar to heavy cream, it's time to temper the yolks.
9. Begin by whisking the yolks in the mixing bowl so they are broken and well combined. Slowly add 1/2 cup of the hot milk mixture and briskly whisk it into the yolks. Repeat until you have added about 2 cups of the hot mixture. Whisking constantly, pour the tempered yolk mixture into the saucepan and stir until well combined.
10. Stir constantly over medium heat and bring the custard to a low boil.
11. Cook for five minutes, stirring often until it thickens to a warm pudding consistency. Test it by coating a spoon; you should be able to run a finger through it without it running. Remove the custard from the heat.
12. Use a fine mesh strainer and strain it into a large mixing bowl to remove any lumps.
13. Add the butter and vanilla extract and stir until the custard is smooth.
14. Pour the custard into the pie crust.
15. Cover the pie with plastic wrap and chill in the refrigerator until it is set, at least 4 hours and up to 24 hours.
16. Serve with whipped cream and toasted coconut.

Toasted Coconut

1 1/2 cups large flaked coconut, unsweetened

1. Preheat oven to 325 degrees F.
2. Spread the coconut flakes, evenly, onto a half-sheet or similar sized rimmed baking pan.
3. Toast the coconut for 10 -12 minutes, until the flakes are golden in color.
4. Cool before using and store in an airtight container.

Toasting the coconut makes this pie next-level delicious!

BOURBON PECAN PIE WITH DARK CHOCOLATE CHUNKS

makes one 9-inch pie, about 8 servings

one 9-inch pie crust, unbaked
(try Rich Butter Pie Crust page 242)

FILLING

3 eggs

3/4 cup brown sugar

1 cup light or dark corn syrup

1/4 cup butter, melted and cooled

3/4 teaspoon sea salt

1 tablespoon bourbon

1 tablespoon pure vanilla extract

2 cups pecan halves

1/2 cup bittersweet or semisweet chocolate chunks

TOPPING

vanilla ice cream or Whipped Cream (page 198)

1. Preheat oven to 350° F.
2. Whisk the eggs, brown sugar, and corn syrup in a large mixing bowl until well combined. Add the cooled melted butter, salt, bourbon, and vanilla and mix well.
3. Set aside about 20 pecan halves for the top and roughly chop the remaining pecans.
4. Spread the chopped pecans and dark chocolate chunks over the bottom of the pie crust.
5. Give the filling another good stir, then pour it over the pecans and chocolate, making sure it's evenly distributed.
6. Press the 20 pecan halves into the filling, spreading evenly over the top.
7. Loosely cover the pie with aluminum foil and place it on the middle rack of the preheated oven.
8. Check the pie after 60 minutes of baking. The filling should be almost set, and the crust should need a little more browning. Remove the foil, increase the oven temperature to 375° F, and bake until the crust is golden brown and the filling has risen in the center of the pie. This may take another 15 to 20 minutes.
9. Remove the pie from the oven and allow it to cool completely before cutting and serving.
10. Top with fresh whipped cream or a scoop of vanilla ice cream.

You could omit the dark chocolate for a classic pecan pie, but I don't know why you would.

Frozen puff pastry is one of my favorite shortcuts.

It's delicious and makes this dessert come together quickly and easily. Blackberries, blueberries, raspberries, boysenberries, and marionberries (our favorite hybrid from Marion County) all work well. You could even go crazy and add some peaches or cherries.

FRESH BERRY TURNOVERS

8 servings

1 (18-ounce) package frozen puff pastry sheets

2 cups mixed berries, fresh or frozen and thawed

1/2 cup granulated sugar

2 tablespoons cornstarch

1 tablespoon lemon juice

Egg Wash

1 egg

2 tablespoon water

turnbinado sugar (optional)

1. Thaw the puff pastry on the counter for thirty minutes.
2. Preheat oven to 400° F.
3. Line a cookie sheet or half-sheet pan with parchment paper.
4. Place the berries in a mixing bowl.
5. Thoroughly combine the sugar and cornstarch in a separate small bowl.
6. Sprinkle over the berries and stir to coat.
7. Stir in the lemon juice.
8. Cut the pastry into 8 rectangles and stretch them gently to make squares.
9. Place a scoop of berries in the center of each pastry square then fold into a triangle. Pinch the edges together.
10. Whisk the egg with the water to make an egg wash.
11. Brush it over the the top of each pastry.
12. Sprinkle with turbinado sugar.
13. Bake in preheated oven for 15 - 20 minutes, until golden brown.
14. Serve warm with vanilla ice cream.

Turbinado sugar has large crystals that produce a delightful texture when used as a finishing sugar on pastries and cookies.

TREEHOUSE MUD PIE

10 servings

Special equipment: 9-inch Springform pan

Crust

20 chocolate sandwich cookies

1/4 cup butter, melted

Filling

1 gallon coffee ice cream, softened

1/2 cup heavy cream

1 1/2 cups Dark Chocolate Ganache (page 216)

1 cup sliced almonds, toasted

Garnish

Whipped Cream (page 198)

1/2 cup warmed Dark Chocolate Ganache

1/2 cup sliced almonds, toasted

1. Preheat oven to 350º F.
2. Arrange 1 1/2 cups of sliced almonds in an even layer on a sheet pan.
3. Place the cookies in a food processor or blender and grind them into a fine crumb texture.
4. Add the melted butter and blend it into the crumbs until well combined.
5. Press the cookie crust onto the bottom and about halfway up the sides of a 10-inch springform pan.
6. Place the almonds and the crust in the preheated oven. Bake the crust for 10 minutes and roast the almonds for 10 - 12 minutes until golden brown.
7. Make the Dark Chocolate Ganache. Allow it to cool at room temperature, stirring occasionally. It should be thick but not too firm. You may make it ahead of time and keep it refrigerated, then warm it up in the microwave when it's time to use it.
8. Allow the crust and almonds to cool completely. You may place the crust in the freezer to speed up the process.
9. Once the almonds, crust, and ganache are cool, make the ice cream filling.
10. Allow the ice cream to soften for about 10 minutes. It should be easy to scoop but not melted.
11. Working quickly, place the ice cream in a stand mixer bowl or a large mixing bowl. Add the heavy cream and mix with the paddle attachment or electric beaters until smooth.
12. Spread half the ice cream mixture in the springform pan over the chocolate cookie crust.
13. Spread 3/4 cup of the ganache over the ice cream (if it's gotten too thick, microwave it for about thirty seconds).
14. Sprinkle a layer of almonds on top of the ganache.
15. Repeat with the remaining ice cream, another 3/4 cup of ganache, and a layer of almonds on top.
16. Freeze the mud pie overnight or for at least twelve hours.
17. Cut in 10 - 12 pieces with a hot knife.
18. Serve with a warm ganache drizzle, whipped cream, and toasted almonds.

My nephew, Steven, often requested Mud Pie for his July birthday, and I loved making it for him!

Acknowledgments

I have never felt more fortunate to be the youngest of six than in the past year.

First and foremost, a huge thank you to Billy for enthusiastically saying yes when I said I wanted to write a cookbook and needed as many recipes as he could provide. What he didn't have typed out or written, he made again in his kitchen and mine. The last two recipes to go in the book were the Trout Almondine and Stuffed Trout. He hadn't made them in years, and I happily sipped red wine while he worked his magic in my kitchen and came up with delicious renditions that would have made Dad proud. Thank you also, big brother, for never making me feel like I was any less than the otherwise male kitchen staff. That was a big deal. Last but not least, undying thanks for the castle cakes.

I can't do much of anything without my sister, Cindy, and this book was no exception. She is the person I trust most in this world, and she was with me every step of the way with encouragement, editing, and validation of vague memories. Thank you, Sissy, for always "getting it" and making me laugh like no one else.

After Bob passed, my brother Michael swooped in like a superhero to take over and facilitate the sale of our business. I will forever be grateful to him for allowing me precious time to care for myself and my girls and eventually pick back up on writing.

Patrick continues to personify hospitality and serve favorites like Tillamook Cheddar Cheese Soup and Whiskey Cured Prime Rib in Eugene at Mac's Nightclub and Custom Catering. I so appreciate his enthusiasm for this book and for being a caring, generous, and hilarious brother.

I have many great memories of my sister, Suzanne, and I singing in the Treehouse lounge and spending countless hours together at the restaurant and home while our parents worked. Thank you, Sissy, for being a great friend and continuing to bring beautiful music to our family.

In an effort to keep things concise, some major players were reduced to supporting roles or left out entirely of the stories in this book, most notably the Cisler family, my nieces, nephews, and in-laws. This has caused me great angst, but thankfully, my dear book coach said I could gush a little in the acknowledgments.

There wouldn't have been a Treehouse Restaurant without Jim and Sharon Cisler, Dad and Mom's partners, who became extended family, along with their four children Coreen, Crystal (my dear friend and classmate through twelve years of Catholic school), Jason, and James. Jim and Sharon have been enjoying life in Hawaii, Jim's birthplace, for several years. It's a well-deserved change of pace after the rigorous schedule of restaurant life  and Sharon's nursing career, not to mention putting up with the craziness of the McCallum family. Jim and Sharon, you have my gratitude and a very special place in my heart for that and so much more.

An auntie couldn't ask for better nieces and nephews. Like me, they all grew up in restaurants and worked in the industry. Sara began by helping her grandma with flowers at the Treehouse, then bartended and served at her dad's and other restaurants before settling into her career as administrator director of a mental health clinic. Steven trained under his Uncle Billy and took his immense talent to Seattle kitchens. Now he cooks for pleasure, and for his sweet partner, Kat, while building a business as a contractor on the Oregon coast. Like her aunts, Cindy and Sue, Alicia's heart does not lie in hospitality, but she paid her dues at her dad's and uncle's restaurants. She prompted me to start my recipe blog when she asked me to write down my recipes years ago, so I owe her many thanks for that and her help with the book. John is enjoying great success in the Chicago  restaurant scene, working his way up the ranks in management, making all of us very proud, especially his dad, Billy. Abby continues to wait tables while working with families using her degree from OSU in social work. And last (only because she's the youngest), Nicole is a successful restaurant manager in southern Oregon who, as of this writing, is ready to move on to her next chapter and start a family. The six of them are as different as my five siblings and me, but Dad and Mom's commitment to hard work, integrity, and service to others lives on in each of their grandchildren.

Special thanks to Linda Salmon for your tireless work at the Treehouse and for bringing Sara, Steven, and Alicia into the world. You will always be my sister, and I'm so happy you are still in my life.

I know Nancy has been with me in spirit. She was a great writer and inspired me with her wit. I see her spark in her children, John, Abby, and Nicole, and I will forever cherish her contribution to our family; our time with her was far too brief.

Randy and Peter, thanks for being the coolest, calmest brothers-in-law. Gretchen, Peggy, and Liz, thanks for putting up with my three brothers and the rest of us. Our family is better with all of you in it!

Special thanks to my cousin, Priscilla Ross, for providing details of our grandparents' journey to Bend and sharing my enthusiasm for keeping Grandma Ina's recipes alive. I hope my dinner rolls are as good as yours someday.

There's no possible way I could name all the staff whose hearts and hard work made the Treehouse such a special place. I tried; it got out of hand because I knew I would forget so many people. Please know I appreciate every single one of you. Thanks for the wonderful memories and camaraderie.

I have received many messages of excitement about this cookbook from Eugene friends and former patrons of the Treehouse and Billy Mac's. Thank you so much for your encouragement; it has kept me going and given me a much-needed sense of urgency to get it done.

There is no way I would have finished this work by now without my fabulous book coach, Nicole Meier. Thank you, Nicole, for telling me my stories would be interesting to people outside my family, helping me with tone and story structure, and keeping me on a schedule. I honestly couldn't have completed the introduction and chapter intros without your guidance and the confidence you instilled in me.

Thank you, Anne Chrisman, for introducing me to Nicole. Also, for the walks with the dogs and for simply being one of the best people I know.

Deep gratitude goes to Cassie Clemens, my sweet friend who happens to own the best bookshop ever, Roundabout Books, here in Bend. Thank you for taking the time to look the book over and give me invaluable feedback before the final printing.

Laura Blossey, thank you for making this past year infinitely easier for me. I'm fortunate and honored to have you in my corner, dear friend.

Huge thanks to Kelly Converse and Sarah Gourley for the careful editing and honest feedback. You really went above and beyond your regular roles as my wisecracking closest confidants and friends. I could write pages more about your contributions but suffice it to say, my life is infinitely better with both of you in it.

To all of my beautiful friends, thank you, and I love you. Your cheerleading means the world to me. I wish I could name you all, but I can't stand the thought of leaving someone out. If you think I'm talking about you, you're probably right.

I would be remiss not to thank my constant companion, Davy, who makes me get up from my computer to go on walks, cracks me up with his sassy attitude, and never lets me feel alone. He's all a mom could ask for in a dog.

To my parents, Bill and Betty, thank you for absolutely everything. You are so missed and loved.

My husband, Bob, will forever have my deepest love and gratitude. He was my biggest support, my best friend, and I know he's been with me every step of the way. Thanks for sending me signs that you're still around.

Finally, to my two favorite people in the world, my daughters, Ella and Hailey Schubert, thank you for your patience, wisdom beyond your years, and unconditional love. I am proud and blessed to be your mom.

A
Acapulco Almond Salad, 61
aioli:
    Garlic Aioli, 100
Alfredo, Fettuccini, 140
almond:
    Acapulco Almond Salad, 61
    Stuffed Trout, 163
    Treehouse Mud Pie, 254
    Trout Almondine, 162
appetizers:
    Crabby Mushrooms, 117
    Ginger Chicken Kebabs, 118
    Hazelnut Pesto Dip, 115
    Hot Shrimp or Sweet Chili Shrimp, 116
    Oysters on the Half Shell, 113
    Pan Fried Oysters, 110
    Sautéed Mushrooms, 111
    Smoked Salmon Pâté, 115
apple:
    Oregon Fruit and Hazelnut Salad, 57
Au Jus, 88
Au Jus, Rosemary Mint, 192
avocado:
    Cajun California Wrap, 103
    Corn Crusted Halibut with Avocado Salsa, 156

B
bacon:
    Bacon Bits, 47
    Bacon, Gruyere, and Onion Quiche, 44
    Clam Chowder, 76
    Cream of Potato Soup, 71
    Grandma's Macaroni and Tomatoes, 135
    Hot Spinach and Shrimp, 59
    Omelette Champignon, 42
    Oven Baked Bacon, 46
    Twice-Baked Potatoes, 126
Banana Bread, 30
Banana Cream Pie, 244
barbecue:
    Honey Bourbon BBQ Sauce, 86
    Patrick's Barbecue Chicken, 177
Basic Balsamic Vinaigrette, 64
bay shrimp:
    Chef Billy's Caesar Salad, 58
    Oregon Bay Shrimp Louie, 60
beef:
    Temperature Chart, Beef and Lamb, 185
    ground:
      Grandma's Macaroni and Tomatoes, 135
      Pasta with Meat Sauce, 142
    roast:
      Prime Rib Dip, 98
      Whiskey Cured Prime Rib, 184
    sauce/marinade:
      Au Jus, 88
      Bordelaise Sauce, 88
      Red Wine Beef Marinade, 90
    steak:
      Brandied Pepper Steak, 190
      Filet Mignon, 187
      New York Strip Steak, Mushrooms & Blue Cheese, 188
      Ribeye, Grilled or Blackened, 186
    stew:
      Hearty Beef Stew, 191
bell pepper:
    Brandied Pepper Steak, 190
    Gazpacho, 74
    Italian Vegetable Soup, 75
    Omelette Piperade, 42
berry/berries:
    Chocolate Dipped Strawberries, 209
    Citrus Pound Cake, 221
    Creme Brûlée with Berries, 208
    Fresh Berry Turnovers, 253
    Oregon Fruit and Hazelnut Salad, 57
    Raspberry Sauce, 199
    White Chocolate Cheesecake with Raspberry Sauce, 232
biscuits, packaged:
    Nancy's Tuna Noodle Casserole, 143
Blackened Ribeye, 186
Blackened Salmon, 161
blue cheese:

Buttermilk Blue Cheese Dressing. 65
New York Strip Steak w/ Mushrooms & Blue Cheese, 188
Oregon Fruit and Hazelnut Salad, 57
Bob's Pancakes, 51
Bordelaise Sauce, 88
bourbon:
Bourbon Pecan Pie with Dark Chocolate Chunks, 250
Bourbon Caramel Sauce, 210
Honey Bourbon BBQ Sauce, 86
Brandied Pepper Steak, 190
brandy:
Prosciutto & Prawns, 141
bread:
Banana Bread, 30
Croutons, 34
Date Nut Bread, 31
Focaccia Bread, 32
French Toast, 48
Garlic Crostini, 35
Grandma's Cinnamon Rolls, 26
Grandma's Rolls, 25
bread crumbs:
Crabby Mushrooms, 117
Dungeness Crab Cakes, 152
Bread Pudding with Bourbon Caramel Sauce, 210
Breakfast Potatoes, 49
broccoli:
Ham or Turkey Mornay Sandwich, 101
Veggie Quiche, 44
Brown Sugar Glazed Salmon, 148
brownies:
Chocolate Chunk Brownies, 206
butter:
Dill Shallot Compound Butter, 150
Lemon Butter, 155
Oyster Butter, 158
Rich Butter Pie Crust, 242
buttercream:
Chocolate Buttercream Frosting, 217
Grand Marnier Buttercream Frosting, 224
Buttermilk Blue Cheese Dressing, 65

C

caesar:
Caesar Dressing, 65
Chef Billy's Caesar Salad, 58
Cajun Seasoning, 89
Blackened Ribeye, 186
Blackened Salmon, 161
Cajun California Wrap, 103
Cajun Chicken Sandwich, 100
Pan Fried Oysters, 110
cake:
Carrot Cake, 222
Chocolate Truffle Cake, 220
Citrus Pound Cake, 221
Mocha Roulade, 226
Mom's Chocolate Cake, 218
Grand Marnier Poppyseed Cake, 224
Sour Cream and Pecan Coffee Cake, 29
Canadian bacon:
Eggs Benedict, 40

caramel:
Bourbon Caramel Sauce, 210
Caramelized Onions, 99
Carrot Cake, 222
cheese
cheddar:
Cajun California Wrap, 103
Cheese Broils with Crab, 102
Nancy's Tuna Noodle Casserole, 143
Omelette Fromage, 42
Omelette Jambon, 42
Omelette Piperade, 42
Tillamook Cheddar Cheese Soup, 70
Ham and Cheddar Quiche 44
Twice-Baked Potatoes, 126
Veggie Wrap, 104
fontina:
Pork Saltimbocca, 176
mozzarella/provolone:
Smoked Salmon Quiche, 44
Vegetarian Lasagne, 136
parmesan;
Chef Billy's Caesar Salad, 58
Fettuccini Alfredo, 140
Hazelnut Pesto, 89
Veggie Quiche, 44
Swiss/gruyere:
Bacon, Gruyere, and Onion Quiche, 44
French Onion Soup, 73
Omelette Florentine, 42
Omelette Fromage, 42
Poulet Bechamel, 174
Spinach, Swiss, and Feta Quiche, 44
Swiss Cheese Mornay Sauce, 87
cheesecake:
Chocolate Cheesecake, 236
Hazelnut Cheesecake, 228
Peanut Butter Cheesecake with Chocolate Ganache, 234
Pumpkin Cheesecake, 230
White Chocolate Cheesecake with Raspberry Sauce, 232
Chef Billy's Caesar Salad, 58
chicken
breast:
Acapulco Almond Salad, 61
Cajun California Wrap, 103
Cajun Chicken Sandwich, 100
Chicken Marsala, 172
Chicken Piccata, 170
Chicken with Wild Rice Soup, 72
Poulet Grille, 173
Poulet Grille Sandwich, 96
Poulet Bechamel, 174
marinade:
Treehouse Chicken Marinade, 91
thighs:
Dad's Burgundy Chicken, 178
Ginger Chicken Kebabs, 118
Patrick's Barbecue Chicken, 177
chocolate;
Bourbon Pecan Pie with Dark Chocolate Chunks, 250
Chocolate Buttercream Frosting, 217
Chocolate Cheesecake, 236

Chocolate Chunk Brownies, 206
Chocolate Cookie Crust, 232, 234, 236
Chocolate Cream Pie, 246
Chocolate Dipped Coconut Macaroons, 211
Chocolate Dipped Strawberries, 209
Chocolate Truffle Cake, 220
Dark Chocolate Ganache, 216
Dark Chocolate Mousse, 204
Mocha Roulade, 226
Mom's Chocolate Cake, 218
Peanut Butter Cheesecake with Chocolate Ganache, 234
Treehouse Mudd Pie, 254
Treehouse Truffles, 202
Chocolate, Tempering, 200
chowder:
    Clam Chowder, 76
Citrus Pound Cake, 221
Cinnamon Rolls, 26
clam:
    Clam Chowder, 76
    Seafood Pan Roast, 160
Club Sandwich, Treehouse, 97
Cocktail Sauce, 84
coconut:
    Carrot Cake, 222
    Chocolate Dipped Coconut Macaroons, 211
    Toasted Coconut, 249
    Toasted Coconut Cream Pie, 248
coffee:
    Mocha Roulade, 226
    Treehouse Mudd Pie, 254
coffee cake:
    Sour Cream and Pecan Coffee Cake, 29
Cooking Pasta, Tips for, 134
Corn Crusted Halibut with Avocado Salsa, 156
crab:
    Cheese Broils with Crab, 102
    Crabby Mushrooms, 117
    Dungeness Crab Cakes, 152
Cream, Whipped, 198
cream cheese:
    Lemon Cream Cheese Frosting, 223
    Poulet Grille Sandwich, 96
    Smoked Salmon Pâté, 115
    Smoked Salmon Quiche 44
Cream of Mushroom Soup, 79
Cream of Potato Soup, 71

cream pie:
    Banana Cream Pie, 244
    Chocolate Cream Pie, 246
    Toasted Coconut Cream Pie, 248
Creme Brûlée with Berries, 208
crostini:
    Garlic Crostini, 35
croutons:
    Chef Billy's Caesar Salad, 58
    Croutons 34
    French Onion Soup, 73
crust:
    Chocolate Cookie Crust, 232, 234, 236, 254
    Graham Cracker Crust, 228, 230
    Rich Butter Pie Crust, 242
custard:
    Creme Brûlée with Berries, 208

D

Dad's Burgundy Chicken, 178
Dad's Sausage Stuffing, 128
Dark Chocolate Ganache, 216
    Peanut Butter Cheesecake with Chocolate Ganache, 234
Dark Chocolate Mousse, 204
Date Nut Bread, 31
devein:
    How to Peel and Devein Shrimp, 154
Dill Shallot Compound Butter, 150
dinner rolls
    Grandma's Rolls, 25
dip:
    Hazelnut Pesto Dip, 115
dressing:
    Basic Balsamic Vinaigrette, 64
    Buttermilk Blue Cheese Dressing, 65
    Caesar Dressing, 65
    House Vinaigrette Dressing, 64
    Mexican Orange Dressing, 65
    Poppyseed Dressing, 65
    Sweet & Sour Dressing, 64
    Thousand Island Dressing, 64
dry salami:
    Salami Pizza Sandwich, 105
Dungeness Crab Cakes, 152

E

egg noodles:
    Nancy's Tuna Noodle Casserole, 143
Egg Wash, 242, 253
eggs:
    Eggs Benedict, 40
    Eggs Mornay, 40
    French Toast, 48
    Hollandaise Sauce, 85
    Omelette Champignon, 42
    Omelette Florentine, 42
    Omelette Fromage, 42
    Omelette Jambon, 42
    Omelette Piperade, 42
    Omelette Prep and Assembly, 43
    Poaching Tips, 41
    separating eggs, tips, 85
    Treehouse Quiche of the Day, 44

F

feta:
- Stuffed Halibut, 150
- Spinach, Swiss, and Feta Quiche 44
- Vegetarian Lasagne, 136

fettuccini:
- Fettuccini Alfredo, 140
- Pasta Melange, 138
- Prosciutto & Prawns, 141

Filet Mignon, 187

fish:
- Blackened Salmon, 161
- Brown Sugar Glazed Salmon, 148
- Corn Crusted Halibut with Avocado Salsa, 156
- Nancy's Tuna Noodle Casserole, 143
- Seafood Pan Roast, 160
- Stuffed Halibut, 150
- Stuffed Trout, 163
- Trout Almondine, 162

flourless chocolate cake:
- Chocolate Truffle Cake, 220

Focaccia, 32
French Onion Soup, 73
French Style Potato Salad, 62
French Toast, 48
Fresh Berry Turnovers, 253

frosting/filling:
- Dark Chocolate Ganache, 216
- Lemon Cream Cheese Frosting, 223
- Chocolate Buttercream Frosting, 217
- Grand Marnier Buttercream, 224

fruit:
- Acapulco Almond Salad, 61
- Hot Spinach and Shrimp, 59
- Oregon Fruit and Hazelnut Salad, 57

G

ganache:
- Mom's Chocolate Cake, 218
- Dark Chocolate Ganache, 216
- Peanut Butter Cheesecake with Chocolate Ganache, 234
- Treehouse Mudd Pie, 254

garlic:
- Caesar Dressing, 65
- Chef Billy's Caesar Salad, 58
- Fettuccini Alfredo, 140
- Garlic Aioli, 100
- Garlic Cream Sauce, 86
- Garlic Crostini, 35
- Garlic Oil, 32
- Hazelnut Pesto, 89
- Mom's Garlic Pork Roast, 179
- Roasted Garlic Mashed Potatoes, 127

Gazpacho, 74
Ginger Chicken Kebabs, 118

glaze:
- Brown Sugar Glazed Salmon, 148

Grand Marnier Poppyseed Cake, 224
Grandma's Rolls, 25
Grilled Prawns or Shrimp, 155
gruyere (see cheese)

H

halibut:
- Corn Crusted Halibut with Avocado Salsa, 156
- Stuffed Halibut, 150

ham:
- Ham and Cheddar Quiche, 44
- Ham or Turkey Mornay Sandwich, 101
- Omelette Jambon, 42
- Prosciutto and Prawns, 141
- Treehouse Club Sandwich, 97

hazelnut:
- Chocolate Chunk Brownies, 206
- Date Nut Bread, 31
- Hazelnut Cheesecake, 228
- Hazelnut Pesto, 89
- Hazelnut Pesto Dip, 115
- Oregon Fruit and Hazelnut Salad, 57
- Roast and Skin Hazelnuts, 56

Hearty Beef Stew, 191
Hollandaise Sauce, 85
Honey Bourbon BBQ Sauce, 86
Horseradish Sauce, 84

hot sauce:
- Gazpacho, 74
- Hot Shrimp or Sweet Chili Shrimp, 116

Hot Shrimp or Sweet Chili Shrimp, 116
Hot Spinach and Shrimp, 59
House Vinaigrette Dressing, 64
How to Peel and Devein Shrimp, 154

I

ice cream:
- Treehouse Mudd Pie, 254

Italian Vegetable Soup, 75

K

kale:
- Sautéed Vegetables, 125

kebabs:
- Ginger Chicken Kebabs, 118
- Poulet Grille, 173

L

lamb:
    Roasted Leg of Lamb with Rosemary Mint Au Jus, 192
    Temperature Chart, Beef and Lamb, 185
lasagne:
    Vegetarian Lasagne, 136
lemon:
    Lemon Cream Cheese Frosting, 223
    Citrus Pound Cake, 221
    Hollandaise Sauce, 85
    Lemon Butter, 155
    Lemon Dill Sauce, 161
    Treehouse Chicken Marinade, 91
linguine:
    Pasta Melange, 138
    Prosciutto & Prawns, 141

M

macaroni:
    Grandma's Macaroni and Tomatoes, 135
    Nancy's Tuna Noodle Casserole, 143
macaroons
    Chocolate Dipped Coconut Macaroons, 211
marinade:
    Chicken Marinade, Treehouse, 91
    Red Wine Beef Marinade, 90
Mashed Potatoes, Roasted Garlic, 127
mayonnaise:
    Garlic Aioli, 100
Mexican Orange Dressing, 65
Mocha Roulade, 226
Mom's Chocolate Cake, 218
Mom's Garlic Pork Roast, 179
Mom's Potato Salad, 63
Mornay Sauce, Swiss Cheese, 87
mozzarella (see cheese)
mousse:
    Dark Chocolate Mousse, 204
    White Chocolate Mousse, 204
Mudd Pie, Treehouse, 254
mushroom:
    Bordelaise Sauce, 88
    Chicken Marsala, 172
    Chicken with Wild Rice Soup, 72
    Crabby Mushrooms, 117
    Cream of Mushroom Soup, 79
    Dad's Burgundy Chicken, 178
    Eggs Mornay, 40

    Fettuccini Alfredo, 140
    New York Strip Steak w/ Mushrooms & Blue Cheese, 188
    Omelette Champignon, 42
    Omelette Piperade, 42
    Poulet Bechamel, 174
    Sautéed Mushrooms, 111
    Sautéed Vegetables, 125
    Scallops Normandy, 153
    Treehouse Quiche of the Day, 44
    Vegetarian Lasagne, 136
    Veggie Wrap, 104
mustard:
    Stoneground Mustard Sauce, 84

N

Nancy's Tuna Noodle Casserole, 143
New York Strip Steak with Mushrooms & Blue Cheese, 188

O

olives, black:
    Oregon Bay Shrimp Louie, 60
Omelette Champignon, 42
Omelette Florentine, 42
Omelette Fromage, 42
Omelette Jambon, 42
Omelette Piperade, 42
onion:
    Bacon, Gruyere, and Onion Quiche, 44
    French Onion Soup, 73
orange:
    Acapulco Almond Salad, 61
    Citrus Pound Cake, 221
    Mexican Orange Dressing, 65
Oregon Fruit and Hazelnut Salad, 57
Oregon Bay Shrimp Louie, 60
Oven-Baked Bacon, 46
oyster:
    Oysters a la Treehouse, 158
    Oyster Butter, 158
    Oysters on the Half Shell, 113
    Pan Fried Oysters, 110
    Seafood Pan Roast, 160
    Shucking Oysters, 112

P

Pan Fried Oysters, 110
Pancakes, Bob's, 51
parmesan (see cheese)
pasta:
    Fettuccini Alfredo, 140
    Grandma's Macaroni and Tomatoes, 135
    Pasta with Meat Sauce, 142
    Pasta Melange, 139
    Prosciutto and Prawns, 141
    Tips for Cooking Pasta, 134
    Nancy's Tuna Noodle Casserole, 143
    Vegetarian Lasagne, 136
pâté:
    Smoked Salmon Pâté, 115
Patrick's Barbecue Chicken, 177
Peanut Butter Cheesecake with Chocolate Ganache, 234
    Dark Chocolate Ganache, 216
pecan:

Bourbon Pecan Pie with Dark Chocolate Chunks, 250
Carrot Cake, 222
Chocolate Chunk Brownies, 206
Sour Cream and Pecan Coffee Cake, 29

pesto:
Hazelnut Pesto, 89
Hazelnut Pesto Dip, 115

pie:
Banana Cream Pie, 244
Bourbon Pecan Pie with Dark Chocolate Chunks, 250
Chocolate Cream Pie, 246
Rich Butter Pie Crust, 242
Toasted Coconut Cream Pie, 248
Treehouse Mudd Pie, 254

pineapple:
Ginger Chicken Kababs, 118

Pizza Sandwich, Salami, 105

poached eggs:
Eggs Benedict, 40
Eggs Mornay, 40

Poaching Tips, 41

poppy seed:
Grand Marnier Poppyseed Cake, 224
Poppy Seed Dressing, 65

pork
  ground:
    Pasta with Meat Sauce, 142
  roast:
    Mom's Garlic Pork Roast, 179
  sausage:
    Dad's Sausage Stuffing, 128
  tenderloin:
    Pork Saltimbocca, 176

potatoes:
Breakfast Potatoes, 49
Clam Chowder, 76
Cream of Potato Soup, 71
French Style Potato Salad, 62
Roasted Garlic Mashed Potatoes, 127
Mom's Potato Salad, 63
Twice-Baked Potatoes, 126

Poulet Bechamel, 174
Poulet Grille, 173
Poulet Grille Sandwich, 96
Pound Cake, Citrus, 221

prawns:
Grilled Prawns or Shrimp, 155
Hot Spinach and Shrimp, 59
Prosciutto & Prawns, 141

Prime Rib Dip, 98
Prime Rib, Whiskey Cured, 184

prosciutto:
Pork Saltimbocca, 176
Prosciutto and Prawns, 141

provolone (see cheese)

pudding:
Bread Pudding with Bourbon Caramel Sauce, 210

puff pastry, frozen packaged
Fresh Berry Turnovers, 253

Pumpkin Cheesecake, 230

Q
Quiche of the Day, Treehouse, 44

R
Raspberry Sauce, 199
    White Chocolate Cheesecake with Raspberry Sauce, 232
Red Wine Beef Marinade, 90
Ribeye, Grilled or Blackened, 196

rice:
Chicken with Wild Rice Soup, 72
Wild Rice Pilaf, 124

Rich Butter Pie Crust, 242
Roast and Skin Hazelnuts, 56
Roasted Garlic Mashed Potatoes, 127
Roasted Leg of Lamb with Rosemary Mint Au Jus, 192

roasts:
Mom's Garlic Pork Roast, 179
Whiskey Cured Prime Rib, 184

rolls:
Grandma's Cinnamon Rolls, 26
Grandma's Rolls, 25

S
sage:
Dad's Sausage Stuffing, 128
Pork Saltimbocca, 176

salads:
Acapulco Almond Salad, 61
Chef Billy's Caesar Salad, 58
French Style Potato Salad, 62
Hot Spinach and Shrimp, 59
Mom's Potato Salad, 63
Oregon Fruit and Hazelnut Salad, 57
Oregon Shrimp or Crab Louie, 60

Salami Pizza Sandwich, 105

salmon:
Blackened Salmon, 161
Brown Sugar Glazed Salmon, 148
Smoked Salmon Pâté, 115
Smoked Salmon Quiche, 44

salsa:
Avocado Salsa, 156

sandwiches:
Cajun Chicken Sandwich, 100
Cheese Broils with Crab, 102
Ham or Turkey Mornay Sandwich, 101

Poulet Grille Sandwich, 96
Prime Rib Dip, 98
Salami Pizza Sandwich, 105
Treehouse Club Sandwich, 97
sauces:
    Alfredo Sauce 140
    Au Jus, 88
    Bordelaise Sauce, 88
    Bourbon Caramel Sauce, 210
    Cocktail Sauce, 84
    Garlic Cream Sauce, 86
    Hollandaise Sauce, 85
    Honey Bourbon BBQ Sauce, 86
    Horseradish Sauce, 85
    Meat Sauce, Pasta, 142
    Pizza Sauce, 105
    Raspberry Sauce, 199
    Stone Ground Mustard Sauce, 84
    Swiss Cheese Mornay Sauce, 87
    Tartar Sauce, 84
Sausage Stuffing, Dad's, 128
Sauté Tips, 168
Sautéed Mushrooms, 111
Sautéed Vegetables, 125
scallops, bay or sea:
    Pasta Melange, 139
    Scallops Normandy, 153
    Seafood Pan Roast, 160
separating eggs, tips, 85
sesame oil:
    Ginger Chicken Kababs, 118
sesame seeds:
    Ginger Chicken Kababs, 118
    Hot Spinach and Shrimp, 59
shrimp:
    Grilled Prawns or Shrimp, 155
    Hot Shrimp or Sweet Chili Shrimp, 116
    Hot Spinach and Shrimp, 59
    How to Peel and Devein Shrimp, 154
    Oregon Bay Shrimp Louie, 60
    Pasta Melange, 139
    Prosciutto and Prawns, 141
    Seafood Pan Roast, 160
Shucking Oysters, 112
side dishes:
    Dad's Sausage Stuffing, 128
    Garlic Mashed Potatoes, 127
    Sautéed Vegetables, 125
    Twice-Baked Potatoes, 126
    Wild Rice Pilaf, 124
smoked salmon:
    Eggs Benedict, 40
    Smoked Salmon Pâté, 115
    Smoked Salmon Quiche, 44
    Treehouse Quiche of the Day, 44
Smoked Salmon Pate, 115
soup:
    Chicken with Wild Rice Soup, 72
    Clam Chowder, 76
    Cream of Mushroom Soup, 79
    Cream of Potato Soup, 71
    French Onion Soup, 73
    Gazpacho, 74
    Italian Vegetable Soup, 75
    Tillamook Cheddar Cheese Soup, 70
sour cream:
    Buttermilk Blue Cheese Dressing, 65
    Fettuccini Alfredo, 140
    Hazelnut Pesto Dip, 115
    Horseradish Sauce, 84
    Lemon Dill Sauce, 161
    Nancy's Tuna Noodle Casserole, 143
    Roasted Garlic Mashed Potatoes, 127
    Tartar Sauce, 84
    Thousand Island Dressing, 64
Sour Cream and Pecan Coffee Cake, 29
spinach:
    Hot Spinach and Shrimp, 59
    Omelette Florentine, 42
    Oysters a la Treehouse, 158
    Spinach, Swiss, and Feta Quiche 44
    Stuffed Halibut, 150
    Vegetarian Lasagne, 136
    Veggie Quiche, 44
steak:
    Brandied Pepper Steak, 190
    Chef Billy's Caesar Salad, 58
    Filet Mignon, 187
    New York Strip Steak w/ Mushrooms & Blue Cheese, 188
    Ribeye, Grilled or Blackened, 186
stew:
    Hearty Beef Stew, 191
Stoneground Mustard Sauce, 84
strawberries:
    Chocolate Dipped Strawberries, 209
Stuffed Halibut, 150
Stuffed Trout, 163
stuffing:
    Dad's Sausage Stuffing, 128
    Spinach Stuffing, 150
sun-dried tomato:
    Vegetarian Lasagne, 136
Sweet and Sour, 64
Sweet Chili Shrimp, Hot Shrimp or, 116
Swiss cheese (see cheese)
Swiss Cheese Mornay Sauce, 87

T

Tartar Sauce, 84
Temperature Chart, Beef and Lamb, 185
Tempering Chocolate, 200
Thousand Island Dressing, 64
Tillamook Cheddar Cheese Soup, 70
tips:
    Egg Separating Tips, 85
    Folding, as in chocolate mousse, 205
    How to Peel and Devein Shrimp, 154
    Omelette Prep and Assembly, 43
    Poaching Tips, 41
    Roast and Skin Hazelnuts, 56
    Sauté Tips, 168
    Shucking Oysters, 112
    Temperature Chart, Beef and Lamb, 185
    Tempering Chocolate, 200

Tips for Cooking Pasta, 134
Toasted Coconut, 249
Toasted Coconut Cream Pie, 248
tomato:
    Cocktail Sauce, 84
    Gazpacho, 74
    Grandma's Macaroni and Tomatoes, 135
    Italian Vegetable Soup, 75
    Pasta with Meat Sauce, 142
    Pizza Sauce, 105
tortilla:
    Cajun California Wrap, 103
    Veggie Wrap, 104
Treehouse Club Sandwich, 97
Treehouse Chicken Marinade, 91
Treehouse Mud Pie, 254
Treehouse Omelettes, 42
Treehouse Quiche of the Day, 44
Treehouse Truffles, 202
Trout, Stuffed, 163
Trout Almondine, 162
Truffle Cake, Chocolate, 220
tuna:
    Nancy's Tuna Noodle Casserole, 143
turbinado sugar:
    Fresh Berry Turnovers, 253
turkey
  sliced:
    Ham or Turkey Mornay Sandwich, 101
    Treehouse Club Sandwich, 97
  ground:
    Pasta with Meat Sauce, 142
turnovers:
    Fresh Berry Turnovers, 253
Twice-Baked Potatoes, 126

V
Vegetarian Lasagne, 136
Veggie Quiche, 44
Veggie Wrap, 104
vinaigrette:
    Basic Balsamic Vinaigrette, 64
    House Vinaigrette Dressing, 64

W
Whipped Cream, 198
Whiskey Cured Prime Rib, 184
white chocolate:
    Chocolate Chunk Brownies, 206
    White Chocolate Cheesecake with Raspberry Sauce, 232
    White Chocolate Mousse, 204
wild rice:
    Chicken with Wild Rice Soup, 72
    Wild Rice Pilaf, 124
wine:
  marsala wine:
    Chicken Marsala, 172
    Pork Saltimbocca, 176
  red wine:
    Dad's Burgundy Chicken, 178
    Hearty Beef Stew, 191
    Pasta with Meat Sauce, 142
    Red Wine Beef Marinade, 90
  white wine:
    Chicken Piccata, 170
    Crabby Mushrooms, 117
    Pasta Melange, 138
    Patrick's Barbecue Chicken, 177
    Poulet Bechamel, 174
    Sautéed Mushrooms, 111
    Scallops Normandy, 153
    Seafood Pan Roast, 160
wraps:
    Cajun California Wrap, 103
    Veggie Wrap, 104

Y
yellow squash:
    Gazpacho, 74
    Italian Vegetable Soup, 75
    Sautéed Vegetables, 125
    Vegetarian Lasagne, 136

Z
zucchini:
    Gazpacho, 74
    Italian Vegetable Soup, 75
    Sautéed Vegetables, 125
    Vegetarian Lasagne, 136

Photography

All photography in the book is by Molly McCallum with the following exceptions.

Photo Credit: McCallum family photos, various photographers, pages 1, 5, 7, 8, 12, 13, 14, 15, 16, 17, 19, 23, top left 55, top 83, 94, 108, 123, top 133, 147, top 162, 166, 197, 214, 240, bottom 256, top two 257, 259, 262, 263, 264, 265

Photo Credit: Billy McCallum/Elizabeth Burrows, pages 76, top two 77, 116, 160, top right 168, bottom three 169

Photo Credit: Bob Schubert, pages 18, 92, 183, top and middle 256, middle two 257

Photo Credit: Alicia McCallum, page 269

About the Author

Molly McCallum is the author and photographer of the recipe blog AuntieChatter.com. She created it in 2011, at the request of her niece, to record family recipes and favorites from her years baking professionally at her family's restaurant, the Treehouse. She has since developed many recipes of her own and is passionate about teaching others the art and importance of home cooking.

Living Legacy is her first cookbook, but it won't be her last. She loves to photograph and write about food almost as much as she adores cooking and eating it. She lives in beautiful Bend, Oregon, with her daughters, Ella and Hailey, and her dog, Davy.

Visit www.auntiechatter.com for more of Molly's stories and recipes.

www.ingramcontent.com/pod-product-compliance
Lightning Source LLC
Chambersburg PA
CBHW060655060526
44119CB00076B/256